HUNGERING FOR THE FUTURE

WHISPERS OF HOPE FOR A CHURCH IN MISSION

DAVID J. LAWSON

ABINGDON PRESS
Nashville

HUNGERING FOR THE FUTURE:
WHISPERS OF HOPE FOR A CHURCH IN MISSION

Copyright © 1996 by David J. Lawson

This book is printed on recycled, acid-free paper.

Library of Congress Cataloging-in-Publication Data

Lawson, David J., 1930–
    Hungering for the future: whispers of hope for a church in
mission/David J. Lawson.
        p.   cm.
    ISBN 0-687-01592-8 (pkb.: alk. paper)
    1. United Methodist Church (U.S.) —Membership.   2. United
Methodist Church (U.S.)—Missions.   3. Mission of the church.
4. Christianity—Forecasting.   5. Methodist Church—United States—
Membership.   6. Methodist Church—Missions.   I. Title.
BX8382.Z5L38   1996
287'.6—dc20   96-6004
                                                                              CIP

Scripture quotations unless otherwise labeled are from the New Revised Standard Version Bible, Copyright © 1989 by the Division of Christian Education of the National Council of the Churches of Christ in the USA. Used by permission.

The poem "Servant Leaders: A Trumpet and a Towel" was first printed in *Alive Now!* September–October, 1989.

96 97 98 99 00 01 02 03 04 05 — 10 9 8 7 6 5 4 3 2 1

MANUFACTURED IN THE UNITED STATES OF AMERICA

To Herb & Joan

To
Rachel Eynon
and
Matthew Lawson
our grandchildren who are
among those leading us
into the future

David J. Lawson

CONTENTS

FOREWORD

Almost two hours north of Africa University, we turned off on to a mountain road to reach Honde Valley. The low-lying valley, interspersed with rolling hills, contrasted sharply with the Nyanga Mountains, which enclosed the valley into a world of its own. Waterfalls plunged over 700 meters to the forest below. Lush agricultural plots of coffee, tea, and tropical fruit, like a patchwork quilt, almost hid the isolated huts and small villages from view.

Elias Nhamo Mumbiro was taking David Lawson home to the village where he grew up.

We walked the red dirt streets of Gatsi to the Reverend Mumbiro's first school, greeted villagers along the way, visited an elderly uncle resting under a locust tree, and talked with the children playing in the yard. At his home, Nhamo Mumbiro introduced his sister-in-law, Charity, and a niece. There he had lived with an aunt and uncle from age six until he left as a youth to continue his education at Old Mutare Mission.

He led Bishop Lawson inside the small brick one-room circular home with a thatched roof. As a child he had unrolled a mat to sleep on at night on the floor. Now the room serves as a kitchen and storage area.

We were refreshed by the shade of a tree beside the home as we enjoyed conversation and the drinks that Charity Mumbiro had brought us. I had met the Reverend Mumbiro only four years before in Zimbabwe; on both visits to that southern African nation as a communications director and editor, I had accompanied Illinois Area bishops on their travels. The Reverend Mumbiro's friendship with Bishop Lawson, however, goes back twenty years when he came to the United States as a Third World Missioner. He had left Mutambara Mission in the highlands south of Mutare, where he taught in the high school and was associate pastor and chaplain during the height of the Zimbabwe civil war for independence in the 1970s. From those days on, he would say to his friend, "The time must come when you must visit my home."

"Across the years, that was a theme in our relationship," Bishop Lawson recalled. " 'You must see where I was raised.' Yet every time I came to Zimbabwe, we had not been able to make this pilgrimage together until now."

The visit in 1994, when they both were in Zimbabwe for the official opening of Africa University, was important for both men. One could see it in their faces as the host told stories of his childhood and the other listened intently and responded. It showed in their walks, the easy way they sat together under the tree, reminiscing from a common heritage of friendship made possible through the connectional church called United Methodist. Indeed, their friendship is one symbol of the bishop's passion for the global church in mission.

The friendship began when the Reverend Mumbiro came to the South Indiana Conference Council on Ministries staff in January, 1976, when Leroy C. Hodapp was council director. David Lawson was Evansville District Superintendent and the two spent a lot of time together. Then the Reverend Lawson moved to the director's position that year, following the Reverend Hodapp's election to the episcopacy, and the two men worked together as colleagues and developed a close relationship between their families. After graduation from the University of Evansville and Garrett-Evangelical Theological Seminary, the Reverend Mumbiro returned to his native land in 1983 as head of Old Mutare Mission. Then followed his appointment to the cabinet of now retired Bishop Abel Muzorewa. In 1992 he accepted an appointment in the Detroit Conference and now serves St. James United Methodist Church in Westland, Michigan. He is a member of the Africa University Board of Directors.

The lives of the two friends have intersected both in Zimbabwe and in the United States through their various responsibilities. Yet Nhamo as a young boy could be seen only in his village and in the small children playing in the yards on a warm fall day. Among them will be leaders in The United Methodist Church of tomorrow, following in the footsteps of the Reverend Mumbiro. The church, his family, his village had given him the spiritual nurture and vision and strength to leave his village for further education. And he has been involved in education and the spiritual growth of African youth and new congregations ever since. As a highly respected district superintendent, he had challenged every pastor in his district to start a new congregation each year. And he introduced us to the incredible hope the people of Zimbabwe place in Africa University.

The beginnings of Bishop Lawson's commitment to and appreciation for our global mission of the church go back to seminary days when Emilio de Carvalho, now bishop of Angola, was his roommate. In their many conversations, both on campus and at his student pastoral charge in Indiana, the American learned of the Angolan's difficult imprisonment by the Portuguese and of the story of The United Methodist Church in Angola.

Bishop Lawson built on his relationships with his friends in Angola and Zimbabwe. But his involvement in Africa after his election to the episcopacy in 1984 was serendipitous: his first assignments by the Council of Bishops were to Africa. He visited Bishop Arthur Kulah and the church's ministry in the hostile environment of Liberia during several coup attempts. This experience led to conversations with other African bishops and took him to Burundi, where his friendship with Bishop Ndoricimpa Alfred began. Bishop Lawson also served on the steering committee that established Africa University.

Before his election to the episcopacy, the Reverend Lawson, as a liaison member from the General Board of Higher Education and Ministry, worked closely on the General Council on Ministries with Rüdiger Minor. At that time the European church leader was president of the theological seminary in East Germany. Their friendship has continued on the Council of Bishops. Bishop Minor was elected in 1985 and served in Germany until assigned to Russia in 1992.

As the church put David Lawson to work as a new bishop, he came to know personally almost all of the leaders of our church around the world. As president of the Division of Chaplains and Related Ministries of the Board of Higher Education and Ministry, he got acquainted with the command structure worldwide, including the Far East and Europe. So he had a rapid orientation to the world context of The United Methodist Church.

Perhaps more basic, the author of this volume was convinced of the immense value of the global nature of the church early in his ministry as a local church pastor. There he found conflicting motivations in the lives of many people and in the life of the local church. He has said on occasion, "These were not healthy unless they were moving from their own centers outward to the world. Both as a pastor and as a district superintendent, I saw the spiritual sickness of churches and individuals who were turned in on themselves."

In his short time as "chief pastor" of the Illinois Area since 1992, Bishop Lawson has carried to congregations, and to readers of his columns in the two newspapers of Central and Southern Illinois Annual Conferences, his passion for what he calls the "compelling image" of missionary congregations with missionary leaders in a global ministry of response to the world's needs. Church members and pastors in increasing numbers are responding to that vision for today's and tomorrow's church.

Across the Honde Valleys and midwestern plains of the world, connecting friendships provide visible symbols and reminders that God raises up and calls forth leaders when the people need and are searching for a vision.

Bettie Wilson Story
The Illinois Area

PREFACE

It has been like an awakening in the morning. In that wonderful land between sleep and fully awake, one is comfortable and reluctant to stir any further. Just a little more sleep and all will be well. Just a little more time to finish that dream. It will take a bit more time to untangle my feet from the covers. But the eyes keep opening, the vision begins to clear, and I slowly see where I really am.

Like many working pastors, I began some fifteen years ago to awaken to a major change. At first, it seemed that the work was getting harder. The church did not respond as in the past. Working harder did help, but it was not the solution. We knew the importance of increasing small groups, that preaching was critical, that expansion of lay leadership in the church was essential, that a congregation needed a caring spirit, and that youth ministry must be strong. The forward looking church practiced it all and still. . . .

In my last parish appointment I awakened to the rapid change taking place in the culture. In those weeks, I wrote in my journal: *It is true! Christendom is gone. To call the parish a mission field is not a cliche. It is an accurate and frightening description. But what does it mean for the church I serve?*

> **Missionary congregations with missionary leaders—a global church in mission.**

This became a compelling image for me and has remained so. I somehow addressed it in every speaking engagement, retreat, training event, and written article. What I now know is that the way into our future is not clear. The form of tomorrow's church is being discovered. What is clear is the required character of the church and its leaders. The new missionary congregation is to be solid in faith, open to innovation, and responsive to the changing needs of the world.

The good people of Indiana, Wisconsin, and Illinois have been guide and counselor for me. What I know I have learned in their midst. The bishop's cabinets of those states were covenant communities that encouraged spiritual growth and experimentation. There is a long list of friends with whom I have spent evening hours in discussion. To begin that list would fill pages. They will read this paragraph and know I speak of them. I will only mention Charles Myers and Susan Ruach as special friends throughout the entire journey.

This book would not have been attempted without the encouragement of Martha Lawson and Bettie Story. Bettie Story's helpful skill as a writer and editor is seen on every page. The book became possible when Martha Lawson volunteered to type the first draft if I would dictate it.

David J. Lawson
Bishop, The Illinois Area
The United Methodist Church
Springfield, Illinois

A HUNGER FOR A CHURCH

You feel it when someone hums an old hymn,
When there is a hint of a church bell in the distance,
When, unbidden, you half remember a bit of Scripture.
And a deep but vague hunger plants itself at the edge of aware-
    ness.

You feel it when it's Sunday morning and you are restless,
When you grasp life's emptiness but know that is not all,
When you are afraid, or sad, or too tired,
And that deep but vague hunger causes a restless stirring.

You feel it looking at a picture of the old church of yesterday.
When, remembering, you know your hungering does not lead you
    back there,
When something seems to draw you toward an elusive tomorrow,
And that deep but vague hunger whispers of hope.

You feel it when the pain of this world is stark,
When you want to help but feel powerless and uncertain,
When you know you need companions whose hands you can
    support,
And that deep but vague hunger demands response.

Oh, for a church that is electric with God's Spirit,
That incarnates compassion, peacemaking, and healing,
That asks more of you than you have ever given before,
Where that deep but vague hunger will find a banquet table.

David J. Lawson

CHAPTER ONE

Restless and Hungry

"I am not sure just what is happening." That is how our conversation started. He was a seasoned church leader with extensive experience and he was troubled. He continued, "Is it discouragement, cynicism, or just a bad mood? Some people and pastors seem angry, some appear melancholy. Complaining and resistance to leadership have always been a part of the church. We used to say it was a sign that things were going well. However, this seems different."

My friend was reading the signs of the times. A spiritual hunger lingers among us. We talk fast and hurry along trying to outrun the specter of emptiness close at our heels. The sources of yesterday's comfort are now empty vessels. We are afraid there may be no hope for us. A good night's rest no longer relieves our fatigue. Life's rewards are not very rewarding.

Nor is there any escape. The pain of the world amplifies our sense of personal pain. It used to be that a person could limit his or her anguish to individual and family trauma. Now, the hungry eye of television searches out every corner of pain on the earth. Scenes come rushing at us until we feel powerless, overwhelmed, sometimes numb. A world of troubles settles on our solitary shoulders.

Swimming in a Sea of Sighs

I too have wondered how to interpret the churning sea of emotions surrounding the church. Groups of pastors speak of their discouragement and fatigue. Increasing numbers of pastors seriously contemplate early retirement. The morning mail contains angry letters from persons using words to strike out over issues that would have been ignored a few years ago.

What are we to make of the cynicism and loss of motivation? How are we to analyze the growing crowd that looks upon the church as just another voluntary organization? Persons may accept or ignore the church, depending upon political bias, pleasure needs, or consumer issues that have little or nothing to do with why the church exists. Others complain of no excitement or clear vision in their congregation. Our church spawns caucus groups with narrowly defined issues and hostile emotions. There is always someone announcing a crisis, predicting the destruction of the church, or naming enemies.

I used to respond to all this with impatience, sometimes defensiveness, and frequently irritation. However, I recently wrote in my journal: *When I listen carefully to the sounds that surround me, I think I hear sighs, deep sighs of yearning. Perhaps they are a hint of grief. Perhaps they are a hint of hope. Certainly these sighs are signs of hunger. Even in persons and groups I do not especially like, when I listen, just under the surface layer of sound and behavior, I hear deep sighs.*

A bit later I wrote across the bottom of my journal page, *I feel like I'm swimming in a sea of sighs.* One senses an uneasy, restless spirit among church leaders and members. Spiritual hunger, a deep yearning, goes unresolved. While many are reluctant to admit it, there is a growing consensus that many of our congregations might be called "ornamental." Perhaps they will break if we put too much weight on them, ask too much of them.

Beware of Antique Chairs

In my youth, a particular sentence would signal that some family member was going to tell a favorite family story. Someone would say, "It's like the time when Dad broke the antique chair." My father was a large man, six-foot-three with a Welsh/German frame. We had moved to a new town. Our new neighbors invited my parents to a social gathering. They arrived after most of the guests. The early arrivals had taken all the seats except a small, obviously old chair. Dad learned later that everyone had avoided that chair. They knew it was a prized antique.

His instincts were right. "No, thank you. I will just stand." But the host insisted. She would love for him to use the chair. Taking him by the arm and with all the force of southern hospitality, she escorted Dad across the room. Dad and the chair went straight to the floor. The antique chair collapsed into antique kindling. This ornament from the past was not intended to carry weight in the present. It is important to recognize when parts of the past have become ornamental.

Church organizations may be viewed in the same light. In every conference or congregation, there are hosts who prize certain organizational structures and procedures. They insist that these approaches to church ministry and mission will still carry weight, are not ornamental. However, in the Christian church we must insist on weight carrying capacity. As the church moves into the future, our mission is central to our existence. Our procedures, organizational structures, prized offices and positions must justify themselves against their capacity to fulfill Christ's mission. The weight to be carried is mission. The mission environment is now in a period of rapid change. We need new furniture. In fact, finding new furniture is an urgent matter. The time has come when applying glue and varnish will not be enough. So urgent is this matter that it is time to pray for clear vision and the invention of new church processes.

The only valid questions are: "What is the central, compelling purpose for each expression of the church's life? What will advance the mission of Jesus Christ?" Any avoidance of these questions is tragic and condemns the church to continued decay.

Restlessness, spiritual hunger, sighs of longing and hope may be God's gifts to us. United Methodist understanding of prevenient grace suggests that we may be experiencing an invitation from God.

I had a clue that this might be true in twelve recent district "town hall hearings." I had asked a total of over two thousand lay persons these questions: "Do our current procedures and organization help us or hinder us? If we were to build a new way of doing things, what would our congregations look like? Our annual conference? What would we add, change, and stop?" These laypersons told me that my questions were not basic enough. Their insistent message was that we need radical rebuilding, new furniture! No matter how skillful the refurbishing, ornamental furniture will not do.

A Parable of Shoes

If just beneath all this discontent, anger, melancholy, and yearning, one might find the voice of God encouraging us, would it not be easy enough to begin the search for the needed innovation and creativity?

I recently stopped by a shoe store. It was time. Someone had suggested that my favorite pair of shoes was beginning to look a bit ragged. I have worn this make, model, and color of shoe for several years. They are sturdy and comfortable, good for travel, walking, overseas trips, and meetings. After I have worn them for a while, they shape themselves to my feet like an old friend. I look at them while I polish them. They continue to look just fine.

When the clerk asked me what shoe I would like to see, I pointed to my feet: "Ones just like these." She could see from the contented look on my face that I was a person of purpose. Without another word, she produced the shoes and prepared to help me try them on. However, the clerk had failed me! She had found the same model, make, and color. But there was a serious difference. She had brought out "new shoes." I muttered: "Oh, how I hate to come in here." Startled, she asked: "Why? Is there something wrong?"

"Yes. When I put on these shoes this morning, they looked great. Now you have placed the new shoes beside them and my favorite shoes look terrible! Worn out. Water stained. Probably not very good for my feet." I did buy the new shoes. But I wore the old ones for the remainder of the day. It is hard to let go of something that "fits like an old shoe."

Many of us belong to old shoe congregations. They have been good places to find our sustaining faith, comfort, friends, and, in a deep and satisfying way, to be in touch with the presence of God. Just being with our congregation is important enough to bring us back each week. Old shoe congregations have a lot to commend them. They help others like us find these same blessings.

However, old shoe congregations have some major disadvantages. The very comfort we value frequently blinds us to new challenges and crippling shortcomings. We become insensitive to persons with different needs or problems. The "old shoe fit" insulates us from appropriate discomfort with human suffering. Our stewardship tends to become "just enough but not too much." When someone suggests a new way of worshiping, or doing mission, we unconsciously resist. Will the church ask us to give up anything, to change or run any risk? The comfortable old shoe becomes our spiritual prison.

The Christian movement has always leaned forward looking for what is around the next curve in the road, asking what new response God seeks from the church. Even a momentary glance at our history makes plain the constant process of adjustment and the occasional dramatic shifts in our life. There are indications that we are now in one of those dramatic shifts. Some churches display the openness required to participate in God's next move. In other churches, a fortress mentality dominates and people cling to their old shoes. Institutional fundamentalism has a tight grip on many of us.

God had a difficult time nudging our spiritual ancestors into "new shoes." We can be grateful that each generation had enough persons of imagination and courage to respond. Now it is our turn! Here are some questions that may help us see these old shoe congregations in the light of God's new invitations:

1. Are persons growing in relationship to God through participation in our congregations? All persons? Say it again: All persons? Are they freely yielding increasing portions of their life to the influence of Christ's teachings?

2. Are persons growing in their knowledge of Scripture, the wisdom of the Christian movement, and the history of our church? Are they moving beyond an elementary level of understanding?

3. Are persons giving evidence of increased Christian commitment by the way they live? How do we know this? What are the signs?

4. Are persons growing in compassionate world citizenship, actively learning about and responding to needs of others? Are they finding practical ways to express membership in this global United Methodist Church?

5. Are persons viewing our congregations as supportive centers of excitement and joy? Are we inventing new approaches to worship and spiritual nurture that are responsive to the needs and interests of unchurched persons

living within our assigned parishes? Are we discovering new ways of learning what these needs and interests are?

The Believability of the Church: Another Stone in Old Shoes

Lest I lead you astray, let me be clear that I believe most congregations are hopeful and helpful gatherings of God's people. Most pastors are committed and caring persons who gladly give themselves in service and love. That is my experience. These good people, swimming in this sea of sighs, yearn for new insight and new understandings about how to be the church. It is not an easy time.

Unfortunately, many persons not participating in the church find it difficult to believe this. An article in *Illinois Times* (March 31, 1994) supports their doubt. It reports that while Americans are quite critical of the media, a recent survey shows that we find the media more believable than the church. The article reports a survey taken by the Times Mirror Center for the People and the Press. The survey discovered that only 68 percent believe what they read in newspapers, 73 percent find television news believable, but only 60 percent say they believe the church. This sample was from the entire United States population, not just church members. The researchers did not gather information by denomination or theological position. While friends in Europe suggest this is probably true there, other friends in Africa and Asia doubt such a survey would discover such skepticism about the church.

It is difficult to accept such a report, especially when there are groups loosely related to the church who specialize in criticism. Still, Christian love is truth-seeking. If this survey is accurate, we need to address its meaning. It tells us something about the general population we seek to reach with our message. What can we learn?

1. First, a basic theological position. Christian love is truth-seeking. The genuine search for truth has never been a threat to the church. We have nothing to fear in the public exchange that explores and raises questions. The church has weakened its own witness in the past with panic and emotionally filled alarm. When we thoughtfully share our faith positions with a respectful willingness to listen, others will be more open to our message.

2. Christian people are expected to be tough-minded about facts. When we write or speak, we must discipline ourselves to check and then check again to be sure of our information. When we listen or read, we maintain the same insistence that the facts are verifiable. Reporters sometimes seem cynical about church representatives. They frequently have good reason for their cynicism. Too often we have spoken with an emotion not supported by accurate information.

3. We evangelical Christians must listen to the real questions facing the world. This will require a large measure of listening followed by honest pondering and further open study. At no point are we more criticized. One still hears the old saying: "Christians answer questions no one is asking." Or again, "For some religious people, listening only means waiting for a pause so they can start talking again."

4. Troubling issues deserve study and reflective debate. Take an inventory! There is poverty in our own communities as well as around the world. There is racism in our own souls and in our towns. Our own indifferent voting patterns are as chronic as the indifferent political and economic systems. Troubled children are awash in an adult population unwilling to take responsible action or to vote money. Sloganeering and simplistic solutions are not helpful responses to such complexity. The world deserves better from the Christian community.

5. Finally and most disquieting, the church will not be believed until it enters the public search for a healthier future. Some of us feel unprepared to enter this search. Others feel limited by too little knowledge of Christian teaching. Others insist that the church should "stay out of politics." Some are aware that values other than those taught by the Christian faith are informing their emotions. Despite all this perceived limitation and reluctance, our times need the wisdom of Jesus Christ. We need persons who will share their growing discernment with humble and respectful spirits.

There is no reason for despair! Wise and able laity and pastors who are more than capable of entering the public debate are present among us. There are truth-seekers with generous and gentle hearts. They want to participate in the search for a healthier future. The yearning in their deep sighs is a hunger for a spiritual growth that will allow them to be commissioned to this ministry.

> I thank my God every time I remember you, constantly praying with joy in every one of my prayers for all of you, because of your sharing in the gospel from the first day until now. I am confident of this, that the one who began a good work among you will bring it to completion by the day of Jesus Christ. (Philippians 1:3-6)

CHAPTER TWO

An Elusive Tomorrow: A Change Completed

A change has taken place that involves every congregation and every pastor. The occurrence has been a quiet one not noticed by many of us. Do not look for it in the future; it has already occurred. The church may no longer be described as a movement with chapels and chaplains, a settled mentality that provides religious services for those who come to the church. In the not distant past, we fulfilled our ministry in what seemed an essentially Christian environment that was extraordinarily friendly to the church. At least the culture of the United States and portions of Europe described itself as Christian with support for Christian values.

Christian people and their churches now live in a missionary environment. Not to recognize this reality is to choose to live in an illusion. The shift is from chapel to missionary congregation, from chaplains of the establishment to missionary pastors. Many laity and clergy must now experience a revolution in perception.

It is easy to say that we must become evangelistic again, to return to the lost strength and methods of our past. But here we do not speak of a "returning." Our principal challenge is to be sensitive to what is emerging in the future. That future includes a new cultural environment: highly technological, scientifically oriented, extremely secularized, and increasingly diverse in religion. Christian congregations and pastors together have an enormous responsibility to claim our fresh identity as people sent by God into new days. They are responsible for outreach that is both sharing the faith and compassionate service. In this shift clergy and laity must provide leadership. This leadership must include study, thoughtfulness, an enormous amount of courage, and a reexamination of how to share the faith in clearer language.

Our congregations are not reaching a large portion of our population. Many of the unreached are not angry with the church. They are indifferent to it. They do not understand our religious language. They do not know our stories. They have not heard of our heroes. It is time for the church to realize that a different world has quietly slipped up on us. This is an exciting moment. Of course, we could withdraw and become defensive. In doing so, we would betray our calling and embarrass ourselves.

The paradigm shift from the settled and secure context to a missionary environment especially involves laity. In their places of employment, school, play, and family, are persons who for the most part do not understand the Christian movement. One may not assume the affirmation of Christian values or worldview. No one else except church members can interpret the faith in such an environment. Thus, an intentional emphasis on the ministry of the laity is crucial to the missionary congregation.

We must expand the ministry of the laity beyond the current and limited interpretation. Many laypersons interpret their ministry to mean holding more church offices and greater participation in local church and denominational structures. Such participation is important. However, such limited interpretation is ingrown and will eventually produce spiritual sickness. In the new missionary congregation, God calls us to provide genuine assistance to members as frontline people, persons commissioned to carry the Christian witness into life. Our congregations exist to empower laity, to provide resources, inspiration, faith development, and support for their ministry.

This exciting, sometimes threatening, dedication to mission grows out of our commitment to study, pray, and yield ourselves to direction from God's Spirit. In important ways we are unprepared to enter this new time. Forces other than those at the heart of the Christian movement frequently inform our assumptions, our prejudices, our habitual ways of viewing the church. Ours is the urgent and exciting task of finding persons who are willing to risk in the direction of innovative mission. We look for persons who will not use the church for self-gain, personal prestige, or ever larger income and status. That is yesterday. It is gone. Let no one help it continue.

This mission affects the placement of pastors within The United Methodist Church. Strategic placement of pastors is a great challenge because of the important impact it has on the life of the church. When emphasis is placed on missionary congregations with missionary leaders, political considerations in appointment making become harmfully irrelevant. Factors such as seniority, gender, or race have little place. Everything must yield to missional criteria that will advance the mission of Jesus Christ in the world through the church. Congregations are too important in this mission to exist only for the benefit of clergy. When we make radical commitments to advance the cause of Jesus Christ, we expect the placement of pastors to support those commitments.

This major shift is also seen in the global nature of our church. We have always been a global church, but our large membership in the United States has made it easy to ignore. Increasingly our friends in the Philippines, Europe, and Africa remind us that in another twenty years or so this status will change. The church in the United States will not be the largest segment of our denomination. We see evidence of that view at the 1992 and 1996 General Conferences. At each of these meetings, the percentage of delegates coming from countries other than the United States increases as does their participation in the process. The availability of interpreters in both plenary sessions and smaller legislative sessions is a symbol and sign.

Claiming the Past and the Future

Some of our life of faith must remain located in the past. We Christians do have a "conserving responsibility." Christianity is a historical religion. Our church must save and pass on to each new generation the stories and wisdom of the Christian faith. Some of our past practices were good and can still be helpful. Someone must remember so that the rest of us will not forget. However, not too much! The vital church is careful not to take up residence among the memorial shrines. We celebrate and claim the spiritual wisdom of our ancestors, cherishing their strong faith in Jesus Christ. We pilgrim people tenderly place in our traveling pack each precious gift they gave us. But we must not carry everything into the future. Some of it has little continuing value.

The present and future must be the location of most of our lives. God has always sought to redeem the "now" of life. The sensitive Christian confidently expects to discover God's presence in life's unfolding. It is the way of the spiritual pilgrim: an unsettling way, involving the laying aside of some things we never expected to do without. To locate one's life in the present and future requires:

• A willingness to live with some open space, not having everything worked out in advance. The desire to be in full control, to have the security of all details negotiated in advance, keeps us tied to the ground at precisely those moments when God is urging us to "mount up with wings like eagles" (Isaiah 40:31).

• An eager openness to surprise. The ancient ones of our faith understood that God gave the gift of discernment to those pilgrims who maintained a "sacred indifference to the outcome." That is, they recognized God had design and timing that were not under our control. The temptation to instruct God has always produced something less than what might have been. Persons and nations who sought to limit or control God were bypassed, sometimes left behind.

• A willingness to accept the joy of the adventurous Christian. No joy compares to the quiet conviction that one is being faithful to the leadership of God's Spirit.

Missionary congregations, missionary people, pastors, missionary bishops, God is now calling all of us. God seeks to teach us how it is to be in the future. These are the days when God is freshly shaping the church for its mission.

Remembering: We Were an Order

From ancient times, every family and tribe had its storytellers: a grandparent, favorite aunt, parent, neighbor sitting on a summer front porch, the tribe's "holy one" whose role was to repeat their history in story. In gatherings of children, around the evening tribal fire, in places of worship, these special persons would repeat the stories of the people, weaving them into heart and memory.

"If you know who your ancestors were and something of their story, you may have a clue about whom you are to be and what you are to do next."

In The United Methodist Church, one person in this ancient lineage of tribal storytellers is church historian Russell Richey of Duke University Divinity School. Dr. Richey said of our Methodist beginnings in the United States that we were a missionary order. With that imagery, he wrote into my heart and memory a piece of our story

(*Denominationalism,* ed. Russell E. Richey, Nashville: Abingdon Press, 1977, p. 172).

We were an "order" within a denomination, an order with a distinct mission. Dedication to that mission created a passion in those early Methodists. We soon began the process of becoming a denomination and this sense of being a "missionary order" influenced what followed. This explains the singular way our church developed and has continued to develop up to the present moment.

Our Methodist ancestors focused on their fundamental mission and constantly experimented with the best way to fulfill it. We were a powerful people because we were faithful to our calling and fluid in our search for methodology. We lost our power when guarding the structures became the center of our interest and we became vague about our mission.

Dr. Richey described this dynamic process in this way:

Expediency, inspired practical improvisation, common sense, pragmatism, eclectic borrowing, the ability to recognize the general applicability of a successful local experiment, the willingness to be tutored or corrected by experience and the Holy Spirit, became the Methodist way.

We build on the foundations laid by those faithful Christians of the past. They cared for Christ's mission and sought to respond faithfully to their own time. We have those same spiritual genes. We too search for the most appropriate way to fulfill Christ's mission in our time. Whether congregation or regional conference, it is important for us to utilize the "United Methodist way."

Inspired practical improvisation. With a clear focus on our mission, we encourage one another to experiment with the improvement of the quality of what we do. We do not evaluate based only on what we enjoy doing or the continuation of what we have always done. Rather, we ask, "Are we meeting the needs of those we seek to serve?" We are open to new ideas, the voices of new people, and the saving of any old ideas that work. When we fail, rather than blaming or finding fault, we ask one another what we have learned and then immediately return to our mission.

Eclectic borrowing. With our eye on our mission, we look around to see what we can learn from other people and groups such as neighboring congregations who are succeeding. Are organizations other than the church learning improved ways of fulfilling their purpose? Can we adapt what they are doing to the church? Have other regional conferences anywhere in the world discovered a more effective way of fulfilling their responsibility? We become a people full of questions and quick to observe with the student's eye.

The general applicability of a successful local experiment. Those who give leadership in conferences look for successful congregational experiments. They seek to share what they find with all other congregations. Gatherings of congregations of similar nature will allow the sharing of both their victories and their unsolved questions, thus creating a learning environment.

The willingness to be tutored or corrected by experience and the Holy Spirit. With a prayer in our hearts, we continually ask the questions, "Is there any way we can improve what we are doing? Are we delivering the service we intended to deliver? Have we asked the people we serve for their suggestions? Are we sensitive enough to the needs of this world in distances far from ourselves? Is God asking something new of us?"

All of this is a bit unsettling. One can only live this way with enormous trust in God and in those with whom we serve.

Spiritual Amnesia: A Blockage

Obstacles hinder us from claiming our past and our future. We assert that a congregation focused on Christ's mission will help its members remember our Christian and United Methodist heritage. We will do this so they can prepare themselves for the forming of mission in the future. It is tragic that many persons are disabled by various forms of spiritual amnesia.

Amnesia of the uninformed: How can they remember and learn? They have never been told the stories nor instructed in the basic teachings of the faith. They may deeply feel their commitment to God. Their motivation to be disciples may be strong. However, when they face even the simplest questions, they must unconsciously rely on secular assumptions and current cultural values. Our congregations have failed them.

Selective amnesia: These persons may have received elementary instruction from the church. They know some biblical stories and heroes. As they begin to encounter the full implication of the gospel, however, they find troubling questions. The Christian faith challenges long held beliefs, value positions they have long followed, assumptions or prejudices that run deep. Seeking to avoid this stressful call, they simply block out awareness of the troubling Christian teachings and passionately defend old assumptions.

Avoidance amnesia: This sufferer will sometimes say: "Sunday school is for children. I did that once. I have the attendance pins." Or, "I do not have the time or energy to participate in worship services or adult study classes." Or, "I never did enjoy reading. I do not want to be forced to do hard study." Or, "My generation does not go in for heavy expectations. We want it light and easy. There are other churches where we can find just that." The list goes on.

Amnesia rooted in pollution: Some pollution is caused by inadequate teaching by uninformed and ill-prepared persons. Some who teach/preach stopped learning years ago. Some use literature so inadequate that our members never discover the full richness of our faith, are never challenged to new levels of commitment and under-standing. Some teaching is negative-based, that is, based on what a group opposes or is angry about. This spiritual pollution puts error and incompleteness into our memory and prevents us from responding to God with Christian maturity.

Amnesia of rigidity: Closely related to several of the above, this form of amnesia resides in persons who are fully aware they do not know, but refuse to admit it publicly. They see such an admission as weakness. It may mean having to admit past error or having to alter a public position. It is sobering to think that we may be held accountable for the things we do not know and refuse to learn.

United Methodist amnesia: The history of our church is remarkable. The stories of past generations, and the present one, are inspiring. Further, in this present moment, a core of Christian teaching is much needed. We must not even pretend that our way is best. We simply say it is authentic and the product of generations of faithful Christians. It is sad that so many people claim our name and know so little about us. Persons may not join us because of our name. However, once a part of us, they deserve to have the opportunity to learn from our heritage.

The reference to "remembering" is so important that it is used 157 times in the Bible. A missionary congregation is one that helps people "remember," free from the obstacles of spiritual amnesia.

Adventure Lies Ahead for the "People of the Tents"

A great "shaking out" is taking place. Responsiveness to God's leadership is testing congregations and church leaders. The choices we now make will allow us a place in shaping the future or will earn for us a place on a dusty museum shelf.

We have always been a people of the tents. We were in a wilderness but on the way to a "place promised by God." For a time, God did not allow ancient Israel, our spiritual ancestors, to build a permanent temple. They were to carry the Ark of the Covenant with them. God's message was powerful, full of vital energy and promise. What is now is not what is to be! This is not the promised land!

Jesus symbolized his own movement toward spiritual destiny with the comment that he had no place to lay his head. With patient urgency, Jesus moved among the people and on through his developing ministry. He sent disciples out in directions they could have scarcely imagined when they first began to follow. Like those before them, Jesus' disciples were "people of the tents." They were constantly learning new ways and going to new places, all for the sake of the gospel.

Now it is our turn! We may not travel to new locations. This place may be our place. Our adventure may be in seeing with new eyes and discovering fresh ways of being the church, for the sake of the gospel. It may be reaching new levels of excellence in our ministry. Spiritual discipline and openness to refreshed awareness of God's presence may be our calling.

The gifts given to us by God may find new expression. Whatever adventure is to be ours, we can be confident that "what is now is not what is to be." God is moving on and is inviting God's people to come along.

The great sixteenth-century reformer, Martin Luther, put it this way:

> This life, therefore, is not godliness but the process of becoming godly, not health but getting well, not being but becoming, not rest but exercise. We are not now what we shall be, but we are on the way. The process is not yet finished, but it is actively going on. This is not the goal but it is the right road. At present, everything does not gleam and sparkle, but everything is being cleansed.

The hunger for adventure, however deeply buried in us, is still a gift from God. The urge to explore the "not yet," to innovate, to grow, to risk openness to the unfamiliar—all are holy gifts and signs that a great "shaking out" is taking place among God's people.

Look into the Future: A Vision of the Church

Perhaps this vision statement will prompt you to consider the nature of your own vision. Certainly, it will give you a clue about why you do, think, and pray the way you do. Each statement begins with "we," for I hope some of you will join me in owning this vision.

When we lean forward, seeking to see around the next corner, seeking to see what God may be doing with our church in the future, seeking to discern what God is leading us toward, this is what we see:

We envision an increasing number of United Methodist Christians, laity and clergy, who are empowered for, motivated for, excited about, gifted for, authorized for, and committed to the sharing of the message of God's presence and grace in Jesus Christ, and who are fully involved in lives of witness and service.

We envision most Christians, laity and clergy, who say: "Isn't it exciting to be a child of God, a follower of Jesus Christ!"

We envision missionary congregations who open their doors and lives to all persons, who love to sing, who regularly share warm fellowship with all who approach them. We envision congregations who surround every person with a circle of forgiveness and acceptance, who make space for every person to grow in faith in ways appropriate to their circumstance.

We envision many missionary congregations who passionately care about persons in all parts of this world, who seek ways to share both faith and food, whose stewardship reflects this passion.

We envision a regional annual conference in mission,

which passionately affirms its purpose to strengthen congregations for their ministry and to connect those congregations with the United Methodist global mission.

We envision an annual conference in mission that focuses on its primary task of recruiting, training, supporting, and sending out leaders for these congregations.

We envision an increasing number of Christians. (Excerpt from ordination service sermon, "Like the Light of the Moon," reprinted in *Central Illinois United Methodist Reporter*, July 1, 1994.)

Most growing congregations are not ideal examples of a New Testament church, regardless of the claims of experts and church leaders. Rather, most are growing because they are relatively young, open, and accepting institutions, with a clear purpose and direction. They know who they are, and they want others to share their excitement. They also are located in growing communities or among receptive populations. Plateaued and declining churches, by and large, have lost their youth, direction, open orientation, and growing environment. If they are to grow again, they cannot reclaim their youth nor their environment. So they must become purposeful, open communities of faith. They must become churches, rather than growing voluntary organizations. (C. Kirk Hadaway and David R. Roozen, *Rerouting the Protestant Mainstream* [Nashville: Abingdon Press, 1995], 66)

CHAPTER THREE

Hungering Demands Response: The Forming of Our Spirit

Unless congregations, conferences, and denominations are intentional faith communities, there will never be a faithful expression of the missionary spirit. Missionary congregations with missionary leaders have no other foundation upon which to build. For this reason, one must start a response to the future at the level of faith development. Any other approach is just another attempt to baptize the current teachings of organizational dynamics.

Prayer and a Pocketknife

The forward leaning, curious, and hungry Christian seeks to form his or her life around the discipline of prayer. We learn from the ancient ones that prayer is one of the great miracles in human experience. In prayer we open the depths of our life to the presence of God. In time, we learn to let go of our desperate need to control as we explore and are explored by the mysteries of God's will. We learn to listen to the profound wisdom of the Scripture, a listening characterized by expanded receptivity to its influence. In prayer, we increasingly receive the cleansing, healing gift of God's love.

My earliest learning about the mystery of God's presence was more intuitive than cognitive. When I was in the sixth grade, a neighbor began to teach me skills required to stay for extended periods in the mountain wilderness of the Appalachian range. For the next several years, my parents allowed me to go into the mountains alone for a week or more at a time. I wandered those beautiful ridges and valleys with only occasional human contact, sleeping under the stars, learning to move quietly in harmony with the mysteries of nature. Sitting on rocky peaks staring out across the great distances, I intuitively began to sense the wonder of God's presence in my life and all of life.

My teacher had taught me to prize a pocketknife and always to carry a small piece of flint. I've carried a knife in my pocket since the seventh grade. In the evening, I would frequently kneel in the rain with one hand sheltering my work and gently scrape the inner bark of a cedar tree, close to the base of the trunk. Then, leaning over to use my body as a shelter against the rain, I built a small nest with the cedar scrapings. I carefully struck the flint with my closed pocketknife, allowing the sparks to land in the cedar nest. Then, blowing gently on the spark, I encouraged the cedar scrapings to take fire until finally a flame crackled forth.

An intuitive understanding of prayer took shape as I learned to see what I was doing. Prayer is like God building a nest deep in the inner center of our own souls, striking the spark of divine love, gently blowing life-giving breath on it until our life is aflame with the sustaining strength that comes only from God. Solitude and prayer keep our Christian life from becoming playacting and pretension. Christian maturity is born of the quiet times with God, searching the Scripture under the guidance of God's spirit, extended periods of thoughtful prayer, and quiet waiting before our Lord.

Our people learn this wisdom from Jesus. His own extended periods of solitude and prayer were critical for the way he subsequently faced life. The nights of openness to

God's spirit made possible the days of courage, service, compassion, and faithfulness to mission.

In prayer we gain a perspective on life that allows us to live with confidence. Prayer helps us to see things for what they are: small things as insignificant and large things as important. In prayer we gain patience with God's timing, not insisting on our own control. In prayer we finally release all of life into God's hands.

These lessons came to me during the long hours alone in the mountain wilderness. After a time, one's feelings of hurry and impatience begin to diminish. One intuitively senses the measured rhythm God has placed in the order of creation. The pace of one's own life begins to move more in harmony with God.

In prayer we hear afresh the great words of Psalm 121, "My help comes from the LORD." Finally we realize that we will never be alone in this life. We can experience any situation, approach any relationship, face any responsibility, look at any failure, and know with confidence that we do so in the company of the Holy God.

In prayer we can learn courage. Courage born of prayer is what allowed Jesus to move through hostile crowds with confidence. In prayer we can learn calmness in danger. In prayer we can learn that our calling is not to succeed but to be faithful.

We do not need to be a saint to begin praying. It is enough to save a little time to be still and alone. We can quietly read the Scripture, allowing God to plant the spark of divine love deep in the center of our souls. With that beginning, we will become aware that we are not alone. We begin to participate in the long and measured view God holds concerning time and relationships. The gifts of courage and calmness are offered to us.

For me, the pocketknife continues to be a sign and symbol. I have used the knife I carry for everything from household chores to peeling apples. At times I simply take it out of my pocket and hold it in my hand, remembering that God seeks to strike a spark at the center of my soul. My pocket knife calls attention to how God can transform something quite ordinary into a sacred reminder.

A Great Stillness

"Be still, and know that I am God!" (Psalm 46:10).

Be still. These words mean more than acting quietly, more than behavior that others would call "still." The verb "to be" has to do with the essence of a person or a people. It implies that one's essential nature is "stillness."

As the reader might guess, when I begin to remember a time or place of great stillness, I think about those youthful days alone in the deep woods of the Appalachian Mountains. However, no one who has been alone in the mountains for very long thinks of them as "still" and certainly not quiet. Sounds fill nature, sounds heard by those who listen carefully. I also remember being alone in many lovely sanctuaries. No human voices. Quiet and beautiful spaces. Yet, empty buildings groan and creak. The intrusion of outside sounds always draws one's attention despite every effort to ignore them.

Finally, I have realized that the greatest stillness I have ever known was within the depth of my own soul. During extended prayer, having read and then laid aside a portion of the Scripture, I am deep in contemplation despite the noise of the outside world. Stillness comes when we have identified our "soul room" at the center of our being and have become accustomed to living there. Stillness has the quality of waiting and listening, of shalom and trust, of love for God. Although one may be busy with the rush of life's responsibilities, at the center there is the possibility of stillness, a calm waiting for insight and wisdom, a sense of peace, a trust in God. I remember an old saying among the mountain people, "That person was as still as the quiet ticking of an old grandfather's clock in the midst of a thunderstorm."

What is it in us that may need to be stilled? A beginning list might include: the clamor of anxiety; worry about circumstances or relationships; a sense of fear or dread; a feeling of impending doom, the feeling that the sky is falling; anger at persons, or about situations; concern about one's own self-esteem; what others are thinking about us; our well-being or our health; a strong need to control life, persons, or situations; the compulsions or addictions of our life that seek to control us. All these are distractions that allow idols and false gods to control our attention and thus control us at the center of our being.

In response to each of these, we hear God's invitation to, "Be still and know that I am God." Out of this sacred stillness comes a "knowing," a sense of poise that informs the chaos of the surrounding noise and clamor. God's invitation, the sacred fact, is that in residing often in the stillness of our own "soul room," where we meet and are met by the Spirit of God, we become centered. The Christian faith teaches us that depth and balance come to our lives when we discover the sacred stillness of meditation, prayer, and the quiet reading of the Scripture. Sacred stillness is a wonderful gift from God.

Dr. Howard Thurman, theologian and poet, reported an interesting account concerning certain trees found in the Sahara Desert:

These trees are not a part of any oasis, but stand alone in the midst of the heat and wind without obvious moisture. It seems that hundreds of years ago, what is now the desert was a dank, luxurious growth. As the desert appeared, the vegetation was destroyed until at last, there was nothing left of the past glory except an oasis scattered here and there. But not all vegetation disappeared; for there were a few trees that had sent their roots so far down into the heart of the earth in quest of moisture and food that they discovered deep flowing rivers full of concentrated chemicals. Here the roots are fed so effectively that the trees far above

on the surface of the earth can stand anything that can
happen to them at the hands of the desert heat and blowing
sand. This is the secret of those whose lives are fed by deep
inner resources of life. (Howard Thurman, *Deep Is the Hunger* [Richmond, Ind.: Friends United Press, 1973 reprint], 170-71)

Dr. Thurman then commented that to the person who is sure
of God, God becomes for that person the answer to life's
greatest demands and its most searching and withering vicissitudes.

"We Are Going There to Pray"

It was lunchtime and we were sitting five deep in the
center section of a wide-body plane. Around me everyone
was speaking Spanish. Each person wore a badge that said:
"Regina Piaz." The woman next to me smiled and asked in
English, "Are you British?" " No, I am from Illinois," I replied.
She raised her brows in surprise. "But, sir, you have an
accent!" To her San Antonio ears, I had an accent; I was a
Midwesterner who had a British accent. Her questions
continued. "Where are you going?" I told her that I was on
my way to Estonia. We talked a while about the World
Methodist Council and the kind of work it does around the
world. Then I asked her: "Are you a part of a group?"

That was an easy guess; everyone around me wore the
same name tag and all spoke Spanish. "Yes, we are from
parishes in south Texas. We are all on our way to Bosnia to
pray." This group of young men and women were in their
thirties. For several months, groups like them had been
going to a church center in Bosnia.

I continued to ask: "How long do you plan to be there?"
It was then that the person across the aisle answered with
excitement: "First, we stop in Rome for a visit. Then we will
be at the spiritual center in Bosnia where we will spend our

days in prayer. We are filling that land with prayer for peace."

This was not a sober, pious group. They were laughing, visiting with those around us, and quietly praying their Rosary. The first woman asked me: "Will you join us by praying for peace for the next month?" She obviously assumed a positive answer for she gave me a small prayer card and thanked me.

By their definition this was a work camp. Their work was prayer. These young adults were taking a month away from job and family, paying their own expenses, and were confident that what they were doing was something very important.

"So I tell you, whatever you ask for in prayer, believe that you have received it, and it will be yours."   **(Mark 11:24)**

Jesus' words are heady stuff! These young adults believed that God would honor their prayer for peace. This attitude is seen in a Korean congregation I know that meets for prayer at 5:00 each morning. Many members are present. They assume their prayer is a vital part of their ministry. Their prayer is in earnest. They pray expecting results. There is no reason for surprise here. Our Christian ancestors believed that prayer was a most powerful act.

What about ordinary United Methodists? Can prayer be powerful in our lives, in the life of our congregations? Can we genuinely pray with the confidence that God will honor our requests? If prayer is so powerful, why do we so seldom pray? If prayer is proper work for a missionary congregation, how could we approach this work? Please accept the following as invitations:

• We know from the Scripture that what we seek in prayer must be in harmony with both the spirit and teachings of Jesus Christ. The work of prayer begins by lifting our desires and needs to Christ. In this experience, we seek insight about whether we can offer this prayer in the "name of Jesus."

- •We have also learned of the power of "two or three" covenanted together in the name of Christ. An individual at prayer is a worthy center of seeking. It has ever been so. The ancient ones also knew the mystery of several persons who combine faith and intense intercession. Experience teaches us that gifts of wisdom and power come within a praying community. Searching together and carefully listening to one another, we sometimes receive the gift of discernment from God. Some Korean congregations are teaching us what happens when entire congregations regularly enter together into the discipline of prayer.
- •This pilgrim is learning the importance of "persistent patience." When speaking of prayer, Jesus used an illustration of a woman who persistently asked. We are encouraged to pray on through the barriers of doubt and discouragement, to pray when hope seems to have deserted us. We are persistent because we trust God and believe God to be faithful.
- •What about the answer of "no"? When is it time for us to say to God, "We understand and we accept? This is not according to your will. We will wait with trust for direction from you."

Now back to the young adults on the plane. I have kept my promise to pray for peace in Bosnia. You may not be surprised that I asked this work camp to join me in praying for peace in Africa. Perhaps the readers of this book would join us in this prayer covenant. Further, I am now praying that God will show The United Methodist Church how best to be servants of Christ in mission. How can we focus our God-given gifts and resources to maximize our Christian influence? How can we create covenant community among us so that all are supported in love and we can be at least "two or three" gathered in Christ's name?

Loving God with Our Minds

If you asked a gathering of two thousand laypersons what they yearn for in their church, what do you think they would suggest? In the district conversations mentioned earlier, I asked this number of laypersons for their answers.

On a short list of leading items was the desire to know more about the Bible and more about beliefs of The United Methodist Church. Could their bishop teach more often? Their pastors? Were there helpful materials they could read? Such questions would be no surprise to Jesus. Do you remember the occasion when a scribe asked him to name the "greatest commandment"? Jesus replied:

> The first is, "Hear, O Israel: the Lord our God, the Lord is one; you shall love the Lord your God with all your heart, and with all your soul, and with all your mind, and with all your strength." The second is this, "You shall love your neighbor as yourself."   (Mark 12:29-31)

The scribe burst out with agreement and commitment. Jesus, obviously pleased with that response, affirmed the scribe with warm assurance. "You are not far from the kingdom of God."

The recording of that teaching moment has given us direct instructions from Jesus. A sacred commandment is to love God with all our minds! Jesus declared this as a part of the "great commandment." We must confess it is a most neglected part. God has given us intelligence and the capacity to use it. We counter that we are too busy and lack interest for such thoughtful inquiry and exchange. God has given us the curiosity to wonder and to question. We have employed that curiosity only in hobbies and sports.

Some assume that they have graduated from Sunday school and want now to do "adult things." Confirmation is more like the end of something rather than the beginning of adult growth and maturing. However, there are signs that God is continuing to urge us to exercise loving minds. The urge to understand has made the *Disciple Study* of the Bible a popular offering in our denomination and in many parts of the world. We see evidence that more persons are reading again. When allowed to do so, our members will dare to raise questions, express their doubts, and offer tentative conclusions.

Our people are intuitively aware of the accuracy of a statement found in the document titled, *Our Theological Task.* It reads:

> Realities of intense human suffering, threats to the survival of life, and challenges to human dignity confront us afresh with fundamental theological issues: the nature and purposes of God, the relations of human beings to one another, the nature of human freedom and responsibility, and the care and proper use of all creation.
>
> (*The Book of Discipline,* 1992, p. 76)

These are not abstract issues. Ordinary human life lived in the streets and fields of this world is heavy with specific examples of suffering, survival, and violated human dignity. The well-studied follower of Jesus Christ gains an earthy theological wisdom that allows for living a fully human life.

What does it mean to love God with our minds? What if we are not brilliant scholars? Are we ordinary people included in this spiritual discipline? To love God in this manner is to read the Bible carefully and regularly. But more, this love also reads and studies the writings of Christians of previous times. Like us, they sought wisdom at the feet of the Christ and recorded their insights. Why always start over as if we were the first Christians? We need to understand what our spiritual ancestors struggled to learn.

.To love God with our minds is to study all of life. God created and loved this world. We may never understand parts of life but we can constantly expand our knowledge of science, cultures, customs, political and economic issues, and human behavior. How? Reading, of course. The library has librarians. These persons can suggest books for us. Magazines and journals can be found in good bookstores. But not just reading. We can also watch and listen. Television specials and news coverage are occasionally helpful. We can observe life around us with the intention to comprehend and appreciate. We can have conversations with persons who have traveled or who study and work in fields unknown to us. The curious mind is God's creation.

Done Any Real Loafing Lately?

The forming of our spirits, you say? Loafing, you say? Yes, just that. When you attend a meeting at Lake Junaluska, it is only a thirty-minute drive to Dillsboro, North Carolina. There you will find the Jarrett House, a restored historic home and a wonderful place to eat good Southern cooking served family style. On the back of their small menu is some thoughtful humor. I share it with you with their permission:

When you take your vacation this summer, are you going to do any **real loafing**? This is no idle question—it deserves your serious and thoughtful consideration.

Over the years, **loafing** has become almost a lost art. In some areas, it is even looked upon with disfavor and scorn. Thoughtless people quote such maxims as "An idle brain is the devil's workshop," and "Go to the ant, thou sluggard; consider her ways, and be wise." This is all wrong—it tends to cast honest loafing into disrepute.

As a matter of fact, much of the trouble in the world comes about because our affairs are being handled by tired men. Our statesmen lack the punch that comes from fresh nerves. Business executives are so weary with conferring that they cannot make clear-cut decisions. The butcher, the baker, and the gas station attendant have all lost their zip. Everyone seems tired.

But we should not let ourselves become discouraged. With conviction and practice, great changes can be wrought. If we all put our hearts and minds to it—if we muster all our resources—if we keep trying hard enough and long enough—we may become really accomplished loafers and thus come to know the restorative value of idleness. We need not be eternally and everlastingly committed to a life of activity, effort, and vigor.

There is an old Spanish proverb that reads, "How beautiful it is to do nothing, and then rest afterward."

Some persons do not need encouragement in the direction of loafing. They get distracted in the middle of any responsibility. They have become experts in procrastination and are genuinely fatigued by noon every day. However, in the Christian movement, we place high value on the **Sabbath principle**. We know the importance of providing rest for our bodies with appropriate sleep and recreation, and the emotional rest that comes from laughter and playful friendship. The Sabbath principle reminds us of the importance of rest for our souls. The invitation is to rest in the presence of God. Besides joining congregations in the experience of worship, profound spiritual rest is available as one grows quiet in the presence of God, laughs and plays with friends, and pauses to appreciate beauty.

Each person needs to find her or his own way in this matter. A little holy loafing. What is natural for one person is not comfortable to another. However, in a time of high competition and pressure-filled responsibility, all of us need to provide rest for our souls. It is one of the ways we can love God. Holy loafing is good preparation for the playful creativity needed to receive God's gift of discernment.

The Gift of Discernment

> I appeal to you therefore, brothers and sisters, by the
> mercies of God, to present your bodies as a living sacrifice,
> holy and acceptable to God, which is your spiritual wor-
> ship. Do not be conformed to this world, but be trans-
> formed by the renewing of your minds, so that you may
> discern what is the will of God—what is good and accept-
> able and perfect.   (Romans 12:1-2)

In prayer we seek an understanding of the will of God. In
classical Christian language, one would say we seek the gift
of discernment. Congregations and persons who would
participate in this transition from settled congregations to
missionary congregations will need this gift. The way is
uncharted. We cannot know with confidence the full nature
of the church in the future. What we can know with cer-
tainty is that God's will is at the heart of this transition. We
have need for continual guidance.

> I said to the man who stood
> at the gate of the year:
> "Give me a light that I may tread safely into the unknown."
> And he replied:
> "Go out into the darkness and
> put your hand into the hand of God.
> That shall be to you better
> than a light and safer than
> a known way."
> (Taken from a quote by King George VI in a World War II
> Christmas broadcast.)

What a remarkable faith community is this church of
ours! Dangerous but promising crosscurrents catch us. The
winsome call of God, the music of God's song, whispers in
our ears and echoes in the quiet chambers of our souls. In
competition, an environment of conflict and violence surrounds us and seeks to condition us. How can one who

claims to be a follower of Jesus Christ find a way through this maze?

The culture saturates us with violence. Drama, news reports, novels, and the Internet regularly present a diet of psychological and physical violence. In personal relationships, we subtly and not so subtly inflict harm, utter words that hurt, whisper tales of poison. Many, but not all, have become too sophisticated to use raw physical violence in personal relationships. Perhaps even more raw is our comfortable use of emotional and political violence.

Many of our gatherings are modeled after the courtroom. Some of our meetings, some of our conferences, seem like criminal trials that follow the basic rules of combat. Others resemble civil trials with the basic rules of adversarial relationship. We uncritically think and speak the language of winning and losing. A competitive, isolating environment surrounds us. We subscribe to rules where the only way one party can win is for all others to lose. It seems natural that we should stare at each other with suspicion lest we give up territory, rights, or privilege while we try to negotiate.

Because unfamiliarity and limited understanding are frequently our condition, we make our decisions based on competition or political advantage—or fear—or anguish—or fatigue—or disinterestedness . . . or too long at the task. We are wooed or forced into decisions that have little to do with seeking the discernment of God's will. Our eyes are bleary. We are weary of the discussions. We raise our hands just to end the meeting. Even important issues and implications lose their meaning.

Still, we acknowledge that God calls us to be leaders in the church and beyond. We hear the call to be sensitive to the presence of God's spirit. We believe that the Creator God has woven into the fabric of all creation Christlike love. Profound, tough, winsome, caring, tender, compassionate love. Standing then with a foot in each of these worlds, we

ponder the meaning of the discernment of God's will. It is
in this precise context that we hear the apostle Paul's word.
One gift of the spirit of God is the gift of discernment.

> **And this is my prayer, that your love may overflow
> more and more with knowledge and full insight to
> help you to determine (discern) what is best, so that
> in the day of Christ you may be pure and blameless,
> having produced the harvest of righteousness that
> comes through Jesus Christ for the glory and praise
> of God.**   **(Philippians 1: 9-11)**

For the Christian, discernment is a noun, not a verb. It
is not something we do. God gives discernment as a gift.
What we can do is discipline ourselves to be receptive to
the gift. On occasion, new insight will come and we will
understand at new depth. At other times, God will simply
remind us that we already know what is required in this
situation. God has already given us the wisdom and ability
to respond. Yet at other times, God will choose to remain
silent and we must struggle ever more deeply until we
finally understand the appropriate question to ask.

DISCERNMENT: A recognition that the church is of God.
It is likely that God has some concern about our discussions and our decisions. We open our minds, all our intellectual categories, for examination by the spirit of God. The
categories we have used to organize life may not be the
appropriate ones within the economy of God and the direction that God would have us move.

Our human capacity for thought, reflection, and contemplation is quite remarkable when enriched by an awareness
of God's presence. We can receive data, information, and
engage in thoughtful and informed analysis. We have the
capacity to enrich this inquiry with intuition, our creative
imagination. We can rearrange data in new and creative
combinations that provide insight and new solutions. To

this natural capacity, God will sometimes add the plus of breakthrough insight. New questions are raised. New categories are created for our use. There is the possibility of our learning something of God's will.

DISCERNMENT: Here is an insistence that we not be rushed in important decisions. We have a liberating sense that external and artificial time restraints such as annual reports and quadrenniums cannot compel us to make foolish choices. We have a freedom to listen thoughtfully to one another with an understanding that the voice of God may speak to us through the voices of other persons.

DISCERNMENT: A possibility when we maintain a sacred disinterestedness in the outcome. We do not propose indifference to the life and teaching of Jesus Christ. This is the basis on which we test all insight. Nor do we suggest indifference to Christian mission or value. Our challenge is to allow the leadership of God to lead us "wherever." By implication we say to our Creator: "Your will is primary for us and wherever you lead we will follow." We make that faith decision before we receive any sense of direction. Otherwise, we are in the position of saying: "God, show us what you have in mind. We will examine it, bring our realistic understanding to it, and let you know what we think." According to our spiritual ancestors, the one who is in a position to receive God's gift of discernment is one who has decided in advance to follow wherever God chooses to lead. With that commitment made, such persons are now in a position to listen for the whispered word from God.

DISCERNMENT: A gift often received in Christian community. Other members of the covenant community offer correction and challenge, new thoughts, and new information. The gift of Christian community is a loving climate where prayerful and playful exchange is possible, where the voice of God is sometimes heard in the dialogical space between us, in the exchange and challenge.

DISCERNMENT: A gift given in an environment conditioned by regular worship, study of the Scriptures, and an appreciation for reflective pondering. A silence, a waiting, a listening for guidance from God. In the experience of the church is found the suggestion that we allow as much time and space as possible for quiet reflection, waiting for insight. We grow still at the very center of our soul, like "the quiet ticking of an old clock during a thunderstorm." In this holy leisure, we offer our concerns to God, explore all alternatives, wait, and listen.

Of course, on other occasions we must immediately take action. We have our tools in hand and are in the middle of the work. No one will give us pause. We must make decisions and make them immediately. In such moments, our urgent prayer may be: "Please, God, help!" If quiet and prayerful waiting before God has been our custom, then in the pressure moments there will still be a quiet center in our soul. The gift of insight, the "Aha" experience, may come as we listen on the run.

> **If any of you is lacking in wisdom, ask God, who gives to all generously and ungrudgingly, and it will be given you. But ask in faith, never doubting, for the one who doubts is like a wave of the sea, driven and tossed by the wind.   (James 1:5-6)**

The Gift of Discernment—Further Reflection

It is possible to use the word discernment as a verb. With this usage we acknowledge that we can discern an answer to a question. That is, we can bring our best judgment, the accumulation of our life experience and wisdom, to bear on a situation. With that resource, we can think the matter through, perhaps discuss it with some friends, and come to a decision. This capacity is a gift from God. The employment of this gift, discerning, would greatly improve the quality of decision making in the church and in our private affairs.

However, as stated earlier, our mothers and fathers in the faith would have us understand that the greatest promise is discovered when discernment is considered a noun. In this usage, God's people acknowledge that a new level of insight and wisdom is offered as a gift of God. These ancient ones, and many spiritual leaders of our time, offer suggestions about how one might prepare to receive this gift.

A word of caution: Our strong need to be in control can turn any such suggestions into a series of mechanistic procedures that, when employed, will promise always to produce the desired product. "Follow these steps and God will be compelled to give us what we want. Do we want to know what the future of the church will be like? Push these buttons and God will tell us. Do we want to have successful congregations where people will come in large numbers and everyone will be pleased? These are the ingredients that, when properly mixed, will guarantee the desired re-action." Life would be more convenient if God were more subservient. However, nothing in the spiritual wisdom of our faith will lead us to such a conclusion. Indeed, this spiritual heresy is enough to distance us from the possibility of God's gift of discernment.

What then can we learn from the experience of those who have gone before us?

1. We have been taught to love God with our minds. The person who is serious about discovering God's guidance must recognize the need for good data and basic information. The seeker will do preparation. What do we need to know about the circumstances to be adequately and accurately informed? Since there are several good ways to approach a matter, someone needs to take the time to identify several alternatives and possibilities. Individuals can do the preparation. However, if there is opportunity for conferencing in the United Methodist tradition, one usually observes a great expansion of intellectual insight and imaginative creation.

2. We must insist that all our categories of thought be kept soft. A spirit of playfulness and creativity will frequently enrich this first step, help us to see what prejudice or bias would cause us to overlook, put data in new combinations, and contribute greatly to the process.

3. Maintain a sacred indifference to the outcome. Across the centuries Christians have identified this as an essential commitment. We recognize that all persons enter the decision-making process with bias, prejudice, and a desire to work for personal advantage. Before the search for God's will begins, the honest seeker makes a commitment to leave the decision, the outcome, to God's direction, with a willingness to be obedient to whatever answers may come.

4. The environment must be that of joyful worship. Those wanting to be available to this gift will be constant in their worship and constant in the opening of their lives to God's presence. A part of the worship experience can profitably be spent in reflection, perhaps with a scripture passage, perhaps with shared readings from other sources, and with periods of stillness in which participants seek to listen for God's intimation about the future and its directions.

5. When the question has been defined and thoughtful data and information have been shared and discussed carefully, the community normally moves to prayerful listening. Prayer questions such as these help some faith communities: "Out of what we have learned from the data, out of what we know through our sharing of the wisdom of the Scripture and tradition, with an acknowledgment of our bias and prejudice, please God, help us to know what is the course of wisdom." Persons need sufficient time to be still in one another's presence as listening and thoughtful prayer take place.

6. After a time, persons in the faith community are asked to share what they have heard or felt during their

time of reflection. They share reflections without debate or argument. The community carefully listens to those who choose to share. Sometimes it is helpful to have open dialogue about what has been reported, to listen for insight and to avoid categories such as right and wrong, win and lose. Frequently God gives the gift of discernment in the dialogical space within community, during the respectful listening and sharing.

7. Humility is crucial. Each participant is constantly aware that God may have spoken the definitive word through another person.

8. One or more additional periods of stillness and reflective prayer are sometimes helpful. Silence is one way the Christian community moves ahead. At the conclusion of each period of silence, persons may share their additional reflection in an effort to learn from one another.

9. There are times when a consensus develops. There may be a strong conviction that God has provided insight and wisdom. At other times, it would appear that God's answer is: "You already know what to do. I have given you the gifts you need. Decide and move forward."

10. When agreement is reached, when a sense of direction is present, then conclusions, plans, and commitments are all offered to God in an act of worship. A helpful question is: "Are we ready to offer this to God? Do we sense we have God's benediction in this matter?"

A series of questions may help as one seeks to understand any spiritual disciplines related to the search for the gift of discernment:

1. What hopes do we have in this matter? Are our hopes sensitive to the leadership of God's spirit? Are our hopes in harmony with the spirit of Jesus Christ? Are we willing to lay aside our hopes if God's wisdom points in another direction?

> **2. What information do we have that seems relevant to this decision? What additional information do we need?**
>
> **3. Do we understand our assumptions about this matter? Have we identified hidden assumptions that may influence us? Are our assumptions valid?**
>
> **4. What are the available alternatives? When we have identified them, can we think of at least one more? What are the two or three more promising ones?**
>
> **5. Will we take the time to discuss realistic pros and cons for each alternative?**
>
> **6. How shall we bring all our data, assumptions, hopes, and alternatives before God and prayerfully wait?**

As Far as the Eye Can See

The forming of our spirits can be influenced by the places where we live and work. Perhaps the forming of the church can come under this same influence. The first time I saw the midwestern prairie, I was fascinated. I had been raised in the mountains and had been living in the rolling hills. Now I lived in a place where the land was so flat it made your eyes ache. I could not stop looking, so much so that at times I would run off the road while driving. The year was 1956 and the two-point charge with 350 square miles of parish was on the plains of northern Indiana. The soil was as black as a moonless night. And so flat! For four years I drove around that parish and never lost the sense of fascination. A question haunted me. What does it mean for people to live where the horizon is so far away? Where you can see vast distances?

Mountain folk

I had heard this matter discussed among the mountain folk of Appalachia. For some, the mountains meant looking up, a sense of awe and wonder at the beauty of great heights. Someone would mention Psalm 121: "I lift up my eyes to the hills." For other folk, the mountains meant always living in a valley, closed in, perhaps trapped. There was a world outside that you could not see and might never experience. These persons felt a yearning to climb out, to take the risk of adventure, to explore what was beyond sight.

In the Appalachian Mountains you met both kinds of people. Some had a profound sense of the holy. A desire to climb, discover, explore, urge others on. And yes, there were persons who always felt trapped and pinched in.

What about the prairie, the land with the distant skyline? What effect does this land have on those who live here? In recent years, I have again moved to such a place. And I again drive across the Illinois prairie wondering how these people would answer such a question.

Prairie folk

Do prairie folk wonder about this? Would they say that the land of the distant horizon means a natural tendency to take the long view, a yearning to see into a distant time and place? Does this flat land produce perspective balanced by a broad awareness of life? Do persons living on the prairie have an intuitive sense that there are other interesting persons and situations out there? Is there a yearning to explore the horizon?

Or, do these great distances create a sense that where we now stand is really the center of all that is? The vast territory of China produced precisely that feeling. The Chinese called their land the "Central Kingdom." Do great distances create limited vision, restricted yearnings? Is it anything like a mountain valley? Does living on the prairie unconsciously create the feeling that the distances are too great, too risky, and the journey too dangerous?

Theology of place

We need a theology of place. The influence of our surroundings is profound. Thus we remember and we affirm that all existence was created by God. All is holy. All is sacred. Walking on sacred ground, we remain alert to signs of God's presence and action. We treat all with respect and are constantly surprised and delighted by the wonder of it all. This perception gives us eyes to see what otherwise we may have missed. According to the Gospel of John, the Logos (the Christ) was and is active in the Creation. With expectancy, we watch to discover signs of the spirit of Christ in all that exists. God's shalom is the controlling design, the master plan, the intention of the Creator. Shalom is the Creator's definition of normal. All in life that works against shalom is abnormal. Again this understanding gives us eyes to see and a way of seeking meaning.

We confess that humankind has corrupted creation. Not all we see is as God intended. When we explore biblical teaching about the fulfillment of history, we learn that the redemptive actions of Christ are gifts of grace to the whole of creation. Christ intends to redeem all that exists. The results of the misuse and abuse of our world are also signs for us of where we can find God at work. Even pollution and scars have meaning for us. God has promised the gift of wisdom to those who seek it (James 1:5). The Holy Spirit is, in part, the wisdom giver, the one who gives the gift of discernment.

Quietly reflecting on the "place" of our lives with openness to new insights may give us a clue to what it means to live in this time of transition. Our setting is not silent. It contains wisdom for those with eyes to see and ears to hear. We contemplate what it is that God seeks to teach us in this place.

Dutch Maidens with White Hats

Rain showers and childhood. Such a good memory. The air had a clean, moist smell. When it rained, we were not allowed to play outside so we stood in the doorway with our noses pressed against the screen door. After a while, we forgot about our anger over not being allowed to go outside. Our curiosity led us to watch. Raindrops were landing on the sidewalk or street. Each drop made a white splash. On a lazy day, there was something hypnotic about watching the pattern of drops falling on the wet surface.

How well I remember! My mother moved quietly to my side and said: "Do you see the little Dutch maidens with their white hats?" In one of my childhood books I had seen a picture of girls in the Netherlands in traditional dress. Their hats were starched white with brims pointing upward. Yes, I could see them out there in the rain, each splash looking just like one of those hats.

Be aware of the words "just like." Even as a child I understood that I was not looking at little girls playing in the rain. My mother's invitation was a gift to see what was really there—and more. She was introducing me to a sense of wonder. Wonder creates permission intuitively to discern meaning and depth. To hear in that scene and all of life the cadence of poetry. **The image was my mother's gift to her son's imagination.** To be honest, I still think of "Dutch maidens with white hats" when it rains.

In college, I learned to see those splashes quite differently. I discovered that they were caused by a small globule of water, traveling at high speed, and landing with sufficient force to splash water into the air. If the drop landed on earth, it had enough force to move dirt. Enough of these drops could loosen particles of dirt, causing muddy water and promoting erosion. This was important information for one who cared about earth science and conservation. However, there is not much magic or beauty in that telling of the matter. Factual, useful information? Yes, but only part of the truth. One could not see the poetry or share in the beauty unless one could also see the "little Dutch maidens."

There is color in an evening sky. One option is to see light waves passing through dust and moisture reflecting portions of the color spectrum. Another option is to see a rainbow and remember God's promise. A child enters the room. One option is to see an intrusive, bothersome, and spoiled child. Another option is to see the mysterious wonder of a small person who models for us the simplicity required to enter the kingdom of God. We see a person whose facial features are plain or misshapen. We can see "ugly." Or we can discern an inner warmth and spiritual beauty. A small choir is singing. We can hear untrained voices and off-key tones. Another option is to hear the poetry produced by great faith and willingness to do one's best in service in the church.

Jesus moved about the countryside watching and observing the wonder-filled depths and subtle beauty of all life. He was constantly catching up the ordinary and using it to point to the extraordinary. He looked into a person's heart and saw promise, value, and beauty where others observed little of any worth. He noted the marvels of creation and pointed us to the Creator. **Jesus spoke of those who had eyes to see and ears to hear.**

"Little Dutch maidens" remind us that the eyes of faith see with simple trust what many would never guess to be present. When the love of God is in our hearts and minds, we might catch a glimpse of what God sees when looking at us and our world. This perspective plus the "wisdom of the caterpillar" may be the preparation we need for insight into what a missionary congregation with missionary leaders will approximate.

Wisdom of the Caterpillar

When I look at our children, mature and capable adults, I wonder if they remember hearing stories such as *Alice in Wonderland*. I read the story so often that the words were almost in memory. I say "almost" for when I did not get it just right, my listeners would immediately correct me. When prompted by this memory, I can still see the illustration on the page of the children's book.

Alice was reduced in size to three inches. She complained bitterly about feeling so unpleasantly small. A nearby caterpillar drew itself up to its full height, which was exactly three inches, and insisted that "three inches is an excellent height to be!" That wise caterpillar could never have suffered the painful inferiority feelings afflicting poor Alice. She felt too small, too limited. By contrast, the caterpillar was quite pleased about its height. Things were just about right. Many of us have yet to obtain the "wisdom of the caterpillar."

Now for some good news: God not only believes in us, but has also given us strength, talents, and capacities for service in this world God loves so much. God's loving message is that every person, with no exception, has a cluster of talents and gifts that represents important strengths for life. This is a part of our endowment. We have not brought it into existence by our own efforts. It is a part of the native capacity created in us by the Creator God. When the apostle Paul challenges us to accept the love of God and become "new persons in Christ," he speaks of something entirely possible for us. We are a gifted people. When we deny our giftedness with such excuses as, "There is really nothing I do very well," we deny one of life's delightful truths. God's love will liberate the strength in us and set us free.

An exciting image in Isaiah 49 gives a clue to the way God perceives us. "(God) made me a polished arrow, in his quiver (God) hid me away." What a remarkable affirmation! Each of us is a polished arrow prepared by God. We are persons God intends to employ in God's own service. Hidden away in God's quiver, every one of us is ready and waiting to be drawn out and sent on holy missions. Our mission is not of destruction but of compassion, healing, and transformation. We stand a bit taller when we recognize, accept, and celebrate the ways in which God has gifted us. The poise that grows out of the Christian faith is, in part, built on the foundation of the celebration of gifts.

"I may feel uncertain, perhaps even inadequate, but I affirm that God has given me talents and gifts of great worth, and for that I am most grateful!" This affirmation is a part of the spiritual foundation upon which future servant leaders in the church may stand.

SERVANT LEADERS: A TRUMPET AND A TOWEL

A powerful image created by Paul.
"If the trumpet call is not clear,
Who will prepare for battle?"
Joyous heart joined with imaginative vision—
Flying high mission's flag.

Then the towel, teaching symbol from Jesus,
Moving drama embedded in community memory.
Savior, sovereign leader, incarnate God,
Clothed self in a towel to wash feet.

No hunger for status, no craving for reward—
Servant leader, servant people.
Counter-cultural, radical, powerful!
Leadership, Christian style.

—David J. Lawson

In this section, we do not speak of the skills or techniques of a leader. There are good books on that topic. They ought to be read. Rather, here we speak of "mode." When one thinks of the spiritual leaders who will guide our church and its congregations into a new future, when one dreams of developing congregations with the soul of a church, one dare not overlook this subject. We need leaders who have clarity that what they share is "the light of the moon." The "sun" is Jesus Christ. We are called upon to reflect the light of Christ in the life of the church. This is both a thrilling and very troubling teaching.

It was Jesus who said, "I am among you as one who serves" (Luke 22:27). Again, the one whose light we are to reflect said, "Whoever wishes to be great among you must be your servant" (Mark 10:43). Teaching by redundancy, Jesus made it clear that we are not to "lord it over others"; that it would be impossible to serve both God and mammon; and that it was humorous foolishness to build ever larger barns to provide for our own security. The servant leaders who will lead our church into its new mission identity will reflect the light of Christ's compassion, gentleness, courage, and unrelenting obedience to God's will. These leaders will not seek status or hierarchical power. They will be among us as those who serve.

Servant leadership is a mode freely and gladly accepted. It is not something forced upon us. That would be coercion and would produce resentment, perhaps even bitterness and rebellion. The follower of Jesus Christ, exercising God's gift of freedom and choice, sees the adventure leading as Christ led and gladly makes the commitment. Instead of coercion and resulting rebellion, the servant leader chooses and experiences the joy of the choice.

Modern culture has made the availability of servant leaders most difficult. Our near desperate need for our primacy of position, a definition of power as the ability to force others to conform to one's own will, and a tendency to translate all achievement into financial reward have produced a generation of leaders uneasy with the teachings of Jesus Christ. They consider themselves eagles asked to lay their eggs in the nest of a hummingbird. Their desire to serve is great but the conditions they insist upon as indispensable for their service are dictated by pride and a desire for material recognition.

The servant leader anticipates the signs of God's activity in multitudes of persons and great varieties of circumstances. The servant leader, thus, is one who carefully reads signs of the times, one who listens with critical attention to all persons, one who reads from an ever expanding list of resources. The servant leader does not volunteer to fulfill the ministry appropriately belonging to others. This leader leads the church so that each person is prepared for and sent out to fulfill his or her Christian mission. The servant leader serves the church by remaining sensitive to a vision of the future that is faithful to God's will. When these leaders announce the vision they see with joyous heart, flying high missions' flag, they serve the church well. A reward for the servant leader has little to do with most of society's sanctions. Joy and satisfaction come from the awareness that the faith of the people is being formed and that increasing numbers of Christ's people are being sent into the world conscious of and committed to their ministry.

The "Dis" Condition, The Power of "Re"

We turn to a familiar hymn to help us further explore the spiritual foundation for tomorrow's leaders. The tune is so familiar that the slightest hint of its identity will cause many of us to hum. You know how a tune intrudes into your awareness and will not go away. This is a hymn we know from our early days in the church. It's the kind one sings without really being aware of the words:

> There is a balm in Gilead to make the wounded whole; there
> is a balm in Gilead to heal the sin-sick soul.

The United Methodist Hymnal is a great collection of poetry. Filled with inspiration and theological insight, the hymnal in its various editions has been a basic resource since the early days of our church. The circuit riders carried the Bible and a hymnal with them. These traveling pastors helped themselves and new Christians sing their way to a deeper faith. It still works for us.

Most of us do not need the hymnal to sing hymn number 375. The lyrics lend themselves to thoughtful meditation.

As one slowly reads these words, refreshing insight comes aborning. Several persons have recently talked with me about their own spiritual struggles. Some were concerned about their local congregation, others about their annual conference, and still others about difficult ethical and moral issues. Those conversations and the lyrics of this hymn come together for me. This is what I found.

The "dis" condition: "Sometimes I feel discouraged, and think my work's in vain."

On some days, not always, others do not share our dreams. A cynic questions your motives and seeks to rob you of your integrity. Someone seems determined to undermine your efforts. Someone else seeks to use you for his or her personal advantage. Codependent persons seek to blame you for all that is not right in their lives and project onto you what they fear in themselves. After a while you begin to wonder if you are wasting your time. Or worse, you question your own ability to carry forward the work needed. You wonder if, in the end, all your effort will be in vain. You wonder and you struggle with the **"dis" condition.**

The negative Latin prefix **"dis"** means "away" or "apart." Who among us has not known those life experiences or personal relationships that depress us and dash our hopes? We are **dis**couraged. That is, our courage is taken away and we are unnerved. We are **dis**armed, **dis**appointed, **dis**eased. We feel **dis**enchanted, maybe **dis**graced, and want to dissociate ourselves from the whole situation.

On such days it is useful to ponder what it is that we have lost, what we feel apart from. The opening words of this old spiritual may help us to give up our denial and confront our pain. Ancient Christian wisdom teaches us that the things we avoid will usually prove to be our oppressors. We are to confront our pain, our **"dis"** condition, but not to dwell upon it.

The power of "re": "But then the Holy Spirit revives my soul again."

The woman at the well learned from Jesus about the gift of living water. To receive the Christ into one's life is to experience profound spiritual refreshment and renewal. In the language of the Trinity, the Holy Spirit is that continuing and active presence of God in our lives both now and throughout eternity. God gives us the gift of strength, endurance, vitality, and hope!

The positive Latin prefix **"re"** means "back" or "again." God's active presence in our lives restores us to consciousness, brings us back to life again. **"Revives"** is related to the Latin word "vivere" (to live). God returns to us again enduring strength and vital force. Spark and energy are restored. We learn that we are not alone, that we are in harmony with God's power-filled movement through human history. The evidence among God's faithful people is clear. To accept Christ as the source of your forgiveness and healing, to acknowledge the intimate presence of God in your life, is to be **reactivated, rekindled** (set on fire), and **reawakened.** Perhaps even **resuscitated.**

James H. Cone, well-known theologian, says that this hymn demonstrated the African American "hope in the midst of oppression." He says:

> Hope, in the Black spirituals, is not a denial of history. Black hope accepts history, but believes that the historical is in motion, moving toward a divine fulfillment. It is the belief that things can be radically otherwise than they are: that reality is not fixed, but is moving in the direction of human liberation. (*Companion to the Hymnal,* p. 646)

The power of God's **"re"** keeps us going, sustains us through the difficult times, gives us endurance and hope. To be a servant leader while the church moves toward its restored mission identity is to need the power of **"re."** Otherwise, we will never overcome the inertia, the downward pull, that seeks to keep us discouraged and loyal to past idols.

CHAPTER FOUR

A Stark World: Spiritual Pollutants

The pain of this world is stark. We want to help but we feel powerless and uncertain of what to do. We dream of a church electric with God's spirit and centered on God's mission to the world. Our emphasis upon the spiritual foundations that will allow us to prepare for such a future can be exciting and hopeful. We despise the necessity to use the word *however*.

However, our faith has never ignored the doctrine of sin and evil. No one needs to lecture us on the spiritual pollutants that weaken our discipleship and undercut our courage. If we do not name and confront these pollutants, we will be as irrelevant and ineffective as our critics claim. Our vision is of a missionary church with missionary leaders. Our commitments in that direction are focused and clear. In Jesus Christ we see tough love, earthiness, and a willingness to face a Cross. We must not flinch when we are also called to reflect *this* light. For that reason, we turn directly toward spiritual pollution.

Yabut

While on vacation, we heard a father say that his son's favorite word was "yabut." Apparently his son was at that wonderful age when children are blessed with infinite knowledge and a deep conviction that parents lose their minds at the birth of their first child. The father's comment reminded me of a rule of syntax: "In a sentence containing the word 'but,' you can frequently ignore all that comes before it and listen carefully to all that follows it." "He is a good person, but . . ." "She is skillful, but . . ." or, "yabut . . . ." This reply may signal a limited agreement or limited affirmation. At other times, it offers the illusion of agreement, the skillful avoidance of a direct conflict. "Yabut" can be a sign that the person is genuinely engaged in exploring alternatives. As regularly used, the word signals that a person is contrary by habit or cynical by nature. There is an alternative behavior to the contrary/cynical "yabut." The spirit-words in Philippians give a clue.

> **And this is my prayer, that your love may overflow more and more with knowledge and full insight to help you to determine what is best.   (Philippians 1:9-10)**

I have been listening lately to see when a "yabut" expression appears in my own conversation. When I hear it, I am learning to ask: "Is it **love** that motivates me in this instance? Can I look at this person or situation through God's eyes? Perhaps it would be wise for me to pause before responding any further and quietly affirm the loving vision God has for all of life, including this situation or this person."

Our love is to overflow with **knowledge.** We can learn to ask: "What do we really know about this situation? Are we watching with a discerning eye? Are there questions we need to ask? And, most important, are we listening? Are we listening with a desire to understand?"

When emotions run high, knowledge is frequently the first casualty. With determination, we select only that information that supports our preconceptions. If we have had a bad experience in the past, the future is seldom free to be its unpolluted self. If we hold a strong ideological or theological position, all the world must bend to our assumptions.

Most powerful of all, followers of Jesus Christ are invited to seek the gift of **discernment.** When we commit ourselves to the way of love, when we seek the knowledge needed for understanding, then we are to wait to be surprised by the gift of insight. Love comes as we commit ourselves to the Christ. Knowledge comes when we love God with our minds and discipline ourselves to do some homework. Discernment only comes as a gift from God.

One distinctive emphasis of United Methodism is called "prevenient grace." By this we mean God's love prompts us to respond to God even before we understand that is what is happening. Perhaps God uses our awareness of "yabut expressions" as an invitation to new spiritual growth, to the confronting of our contrary and cynical nature.

Onomatopoeia

This fascinating word introduces us to another spiritual pollutant. **Onomatopoeia** refers to the formation of words in imitation of natural sounds, such as "arf, arf," "meow," "pop," "buzz," or "hiss." Why would we have such interest in unusual words? Why this trip through the dictionary? The answer is found in Philippians 2:14-15.

> Do all things without murmuring or arguing, so that you may be blameless and innocent, children of God without blemish in the midst of a crooked and perverse generation, in which you shine like stars in the world.

The word "murmuring" is an example of onomatopoeia. Meanings of murmuring include: complaining, grousing, grumbling, muttering, mumbling, whispering, whimpering. But wait! We have yet to see the full meaning of the term. It is not just the definition of the word but how it is spoken. The clue is in the sound.

The sound is murmurmurmurmur .... It is highly descriptive of the behavior. It is not just complaining but complaining constantly, quietly, pervasively, and in the background.

Murmuring infects conversations, group decisions, and social relationships with a critical mind-set. This person, this group, constantly undercuts possibility, detracts from hope, and raises doubt. Like the sound of a mosquito in your bedroom at night . . . buzzzzzzz . . . this critical murmuring is bothersome and allows for little defense. Murmuring persons contaminate with their negative influence. There are entire congregations whose ethos seems a pervasive discontent. Persons who join them are soon drawn into the murmuring spirit. There are parachurch groups whose self-chosen role is that of the complainer, either discovering fault or manufacturing it to maintain the loyalty of their followers.

In Paul's letter to the Philippians, he urges that we avoid the murmuring spirit, for it prevents persons and congregations from being blameless and innocent children of God. Murmuring spirits in the congregation at Philippi were eroding the faithfulness of others, which is the basis of genuine Christian congregation. Can there ever be freedom from the burden of murmuring? Perhaps, but it will not come easily.

Freedom notes

1. The only useful focus is for us to focus on our own freedom from the murmuring spirit. As in other areas, so here, too, our responsibility is not to change other persons or other groups. We must finally conclude that we can do little to change a murmurer, unless we are the murmurer. We may eventually modify this pervasive climate in church and society if we address our own tendency toward a complaining spirit. This awareness is itself a gift from God, a gift John Wesley called prevenient grace.

2. We find our freedom from the murmuring spirit in having the same mind that was in Christ Jesus. That is, we view ourselves and others as loved by God and worthy of respect. We accept Christ's standard of servanthood as the goal of our life. The needs of other persons become increasingly important to us. The more we understand that God has blessed our own life, the more we can live as a blessing to others. As we are released from self-obsession we are also released from the dominance of a critical mind-set.

3. Our freedom from the murmuring spirit is given through participation in Christian community. We need a faith community that will sustain our growth and keep us from reverting to self-idolatry. Today there is a great hunger for such community. Yet many congregations are uncertain how to provide it, and many of us resist it when it is offered.

Paul describes Christian community as "being of the same mind, sharing in the same love, being in full accord and of one mind." Our freedom from murmuring is found in a Christian community where we commit ourselves to unity in Christ. The two words "in Christ" are the key. Any other basis for our unity encourages us to participate in the critical and cynical spirit of many volunteer organizations and most workplaces. In Christian community, while we will disagree, experience distrust, and be angry, we will let nothing alienate us from one another in Christ's spirit. Respect, courtesy, and mutual support are normal for us. We will seek to celebrate one another and patiently offer love and reconciliation.

The New Testament sees the murmuring spirit as a poison that seeks to displace appropriate self-love with self-idolatry, which undercuts compassionate servanthood and despoils the very faith community Christ is building. Paul named it a major spiritual threat. Its unchallenged presence is like a vicious virus that destroys the structure of the body.

Trashing

The trashing of other persons is a spiritual pollutant increasingly present in the life of the church and in our society. I saw an example recently as I waited in line at a gas station to pay the cashier. A young boy of about fifth grade level walked to the counter with obvious confidence. I had watched as his mother had allowed him to fill the tank with gas. Now he held the exact amount, ten dollars, to pay his bill. Pride radiated from every pore. The line was long and only a harassed manager was working. "Which pump?" The boy answered: "Number six."

Glancing at the meter, the manager did not look up when he said: "Sixteen dollars." There was a confused hesitation. Then the boy said: "No, sir, ten dollars." The manager impatiently shook his head and said: "No, sixteen dollars." The boy obviously did not know what to do or say and said nothing. The manager growled, "What color is the car?" The answer, "Blue." The boy tried to regain his confidence, but it did not work. The manager's sharp reply: "You were at number two pump! O.K.! Give me your ten dollars."

The ten-dollar bill moved quickly across the counter and the boy, with a beet-red face, looked at the floor as he hurried out of the station and got into the car with his mother. The manager looked at me and muttered: "Some people just cannot get it right." The expression on his face said, "Dumb kid!" All I could think to say was: "You embarrassed that kid. He was blushing when he went out the door." Since I was an adult customer, the man attempted an excuse and apology. However, the damage was done. The trashing was complete, leaving only spoiled joy. There seemed nothing I could do to repair a moment of pollution. A few minutes later, I said to my wife: "That child will never forget that experience. He will remember that he felt like a failure in front of a line of adults. What had started as a proud moment ended in shame."

We must confess to being in the "trasher's" role far too often. That scene is played out repeatedly as persons have expressed their anger, fear, or fatigue. Filled with ourselves, absorbed with our private agendas, taking care of ourselves or our group, we ride roughshod over other persons, labeling them the enemy and assigning to them motive and attitudes that really find their origin in our own feelings and our own prejudices.

The words in the "Christian manifesto" can serve as a helpful antidote (1 Corinthians 13:4-7). There are words like:

1. Kind: That is, compassionate, generous, considerate, gentle.

2. Not arrogant: That is, not haughty or disdainful.

3. Not rude: That is, not curt, brusque, or inconsiderate.

4. Not resentful: That is, not bitter, unforgiving, or hostile.

At the center is our calling to share the love we have received from Christ, to build up rather than to tear down. To support and encourage rather than to leave scars. To address issues and maintain respect for persons. To leave a trail of blessing rather than pain. To extend to others the same patience and generosity we pray they will extend to us. To see in one another the presence of Christ struggling to find expression.

It is painful indeed to see the trashing of a child in a gas station. It is yet more painful when the trashing of persons takes place in the church. The wisdom of our spiritual ancestors is also ours. If we "do not have love, we are nothing."

An additional thought: What of those persons and organizations who trash the church?

An Old Wisdom Saying

Dusk of evening settled as two men drove along a state highway. They had talked earnestly for some time. The conversation was hushed and serious. Finally, the driver spoke with a deep and quiet voice, "Remember, the dog that carries a bone to you will also carry one away." The one speaking those words was my father. I had shared information with him from one of my work associates. My father's reply was a word of caution, perhaps warning.

He spoke a "wisdom saying" of our family. I had heard the expression since I was a young boy. I would hear it again several times before my father's death. He had learned the wisdom saying from his parents. His further words of caution went something like this, "A carrier of tales is a carrier of tales. Listen respectfully. You may learn something important. However, hold the words in memory only tentatively until they can be verified by observation or additional information. And remember, the person will quote you, whatever your response."

The New Testament book of James referred to the unbridled tongue as slippery and dangerous. One ancient writer suggested that spoken words are like feathers, scattered through a community on a windy day. Try as one might, one cannot go back and pick them up again. The wind will scatter them beyond recovery (James 3:5). I remember my father, John, and a New Testament writer, James, and reflect on these things:

- Love is truth-seeking. Love knows the harmfulness, the polluting nature, of error and half-truth. The loving person seeks to understand life and information as accurately as possible. Inaccurate or deliberately falsified information may be acted upon, thus causing real mischief. Each of us tenderly carries the good name and reputation of all the persons about us. The loving person considers this a sacred trust.
- The more harmful the rumor, the more seductive the temptation to pass it on. Spiritual pollution grows. Loving persons ponder the consequence before even a truthful story is repeated and frequently allow gossip to stop with them. One of the general rules of The United Methodist Church is, "Do no harm."
- Some words are deliberately shared so that they will be passed along. For instance, the most powerful and supportive compliment is the secondhand one, the compliment overheard. Words of appreciation and

affirmation are shared with a joyful heart. In addition, honest feedback, words of caution, or needed correction are shared in love and privacy, even at the risk of hurting a relationship. Most of us are blessed with close friends who are willing to give constructive criticism, suggestions that have prevented us from committing major errors. When what they share is painful, we can receive their counsel because we trust their motives.

- It is important to recognize some persons as "microphones." When you talk with them, you are making an announcement to the world. We do not want to avoid conversation with these persons. We simply will be very thoughtful about what we say. Love seeks to be perceptive and wise, thus curtailing the spread of spiritual pollution.

Smallness of Spirit

Here is another contagious negative attribute. A few years ago, in response to an urgent request for a conversation, I agreed to meet some persons halfway between our towns. To my sorrow, their issues were self-serving, their anxiety centered on matters of personal ambition, their anger rested on perceived but petty offenses. Intellectually they seemed aware of a larger world and the needs of others. Emotionally, a world of their own hungers and greed confined them. Lives of considerable promise were being squeezed into a mean cage.

While driving home that day, I impulsively placed a blank sheet of paper on the car seat. With one hand on the steering wheel, I wrote words that raced to consciousness, a simple statement that grew out of my heart. At the first writing, the beginning word was "your." Upon later reflection, I knew I had to change that word to "our." Here is what I wrote:

> Our smallness of spirit
> is not a private affair.
> It invades the lives of others,
> leaving grief and wounds there.

Smallness of spirit is one of the most contagious of all human attributes. Persons who associate with such small-spirited ones usually begin to mirror that same attitude in their own lives. Small-spirited persons create pools of small-spiritedness. The infection continues to spread, polluting our relationship with God and turning us away from compassionate living. Entire congregations frequently begin to mirror this sickness.

How does a congregation or an individual repent of this sickness, that is, turn away from it? Is there any cure for this spiritual malignancy? We pray so. This virus works in direct contradiction to this vision of a missionary congregation with missionary leaders. Here are some clues:

1. Change the nature of our prayer life: Archbishop William Temple put the matter this way, "We must begin with prayer, because if you are selfish in your prayers there is not much hope that you will be really unselfish anywhere else." Liberating prayer contains both confession and passionate intercession for others. It is a powerful beginning.

2. Slow and careful study of the life and teachings of Jesus: One begins with the teachings of Jesus. An individual or a study group may spend time examining the meaning of such teachings as, "For those who want to save their life will lose it, and those who lose their life for my sake will find it."

3. Reflection on the nature of Christian love: Love reaches its maturity when it is a reflection of God's love. God loves us unconditionally and charges us to so love this world. That is, we are to express forgiveness and care to all persons in all circumstances. Further, ours is to be a neighbor-centered love of self. We care for ourselves and grow in our faith in order to be of service to our neighbor. We infect ourselves with a deadly spiritual sickness when we turn in on ourselves.

4. Begin immediately to participate in both hands-on and financial mission: We lay aside all contrary feelings and identify specific and practical ways to give ourselves to the needs of others. Congregations seek to involve increasing numbers of their members in both local and global mission activity. Without this ingredient, there can be no cure of the soul.

Here is a basic Christian premise. Whether by a person or congregation, the turning in on self produces spiritual sickness unto death. Most of what is done in the name of survival or self-protection eventually proves to be the first steps to destruction. We must address this spiritual sickness with courage and compassion if we are to have missionary congregations with missionary pastors.

Bone Tired

We will all recognize this pollutant. Reflection on it caused me to remember an early day in my working career. I was working on a railroad. The train dispatcher always gave a concise message. "There is a wreck at milepost—! The engine and (number) cars are on the ground. I have called the work train. Who from your office will be on it?" That signaled all of us to drop whatever we were doing and head for the wreck. The priority on our division of the railroad was fast freight. From the moment of that first call until the main line was back in service, no one would rest or sleep.

Meals were prepared on the work train and served at the site. Not to worry if you were wearing a suit that day. The supply car carried work clothes and boots. Wreckage clearance was exciting for a young man. However, I have never known greater fatigue. After forty hours of continuous hard work, we were so weak that picking up a tool from the ground was almost too much. This was a dangerous time. Emotions were on edge and judgment was suspect at best.

I recalled that fatigue recently during a phone conversation with a troubled church member. She told me a story of continuous crisis: Sexual harassment from a neighbor. A husband who refused to believe her. A teenager acting out her anger at school. Enough! She phoned me because her father had just called to say that her mother was facing surgery. Her father wanted her to come and be at the bedside.

At this breaking point, this good person did not speak of anger or fear. She said, "I am bone tired. So tired I cannot think or feel. What am I to do?" I heard the feeling and remembered: **Forty hours of continuous work and no relief in sight!**

It was not a moment of superficial advice. She was traveling on Job's road and had every right to cry out in protest. "Please, enough! God, I cannot cope!" This bishop knew from experience that God would not desert her. Help would come. She would know comfort and hope. In due time, I would assure her of these truths. Now all I could do was listen and let her know she was not alone.

Grief is felt as fatigue. Anger becomes fatigue. Hurt becomes a tiring burden. Pain uses great portions of energy and leaves us exhausted. Disappointment gnaws at us, stealing our bright edges and leaving us hungry for hope. At some point in this "bone tiredness," we may hear these nourishing words whispered deep in our souls:

> "Come to me, all you that are weary and are carrying heavy burdens, and I will give you rest. Take my yoke upon you, and learn from me; for I am gentle and humble in heart, and you will find rest for your souls. For my yoke is easy, and my burden is light."   (Matthew 11:28-30)

This phone conversation led me to another source of nourishment. I finally located this prayer by Dr. Howard Thurman:

> We ask of Thee, O God, no miracles, no vast upturning of life in startling dimensions; we seek simple assurance that will absorb the weariness of the daily round, that will give lift to the ordinary way, confident, our Father, that Thou art very close to us, closer than breathing. Tutor us, that we may trust Thy nearness and be lifted up and

strengthened. (Howard Thurman, *The Centering Moment* [Richmond, Ind.: Friends United Press, 1980])

We yearn for a new and fresh day in the life of the church. We are restless and hungry for a sense of direction. These are transitional times. We have a sense of the goal. We have only limited understanding of how to reach it. Finally, the spiritual pollutant of fatigue, deep emotional and spiritual fatigue, begins to wear us down. Precisely at these moments we listen with open attention to the words: "Come to me, all you that are weary and are carrying heavy burdens, and I will give you rest."

A Preoccupation with the Short Term

This pollution is hard to recognize for it is so natural. Perhaps this will help clarify it: Many questions plague us. Do we vote for immediate satisfaction or long-term needs? Will it be another hot fudge sundae just this once or a disciplined loyalty to a weight control program? Will it be a relaxed attitude to money management or a saving and investment program with an eye toward retirement? Shall I drive this car another year and suffer with "new car fever"? Or shall I take a test drive in my dream automobile and enjoy the "new car smell"? Some questions we face are large and dramatic. Most are small choices made without reflection. The consequences of our decisions accumulate over time, one small effect added to a growing total. It would be tempting to suggest that the total consequence will finally become obvious and we will make the needed adjustments and changes. In truth, we become so accustomed to our life-trend that the eventual repercussions can go unnoticed until it is too late to recover.

The title of this section is a quotation from a new book. One paragraph in particular helped me to name my own continual struggle with the tension between immediate problems and needs versus long-term goals and consequences. The quotation may be helpful to others. John Paulos writes:

> Even the most superficial reading of a newspaper reveals an important aspect of human psychology: our preoccupation with the short term. Essential to our survival, our myopic focus on the day's happenings can nevertheless cause problems for us. Evolution's favoring of organisms that respond to local or near-term events results in a steep temporal and spatial discount rate for distant or future events. The latter are discounted in the same way that money is. Suffering ordained for twenty years from now is, like a million-dollar debt due in twenty years, considerably easier to bear than is suffering scheduled for tomorrow. (John Allen Paulos, *A Mathematician Reads the Newspaper* [New York: Basic Books, 1995], 96)

When the harm of a behavior is not due for payment until a distant future, we discount its importance. If the effect of an action is felt only by persons geographically distant from us, we tend not to feel personal responsibility. Even in the church we make choices that have the appearance of a Ponzi operation:

> In a Ponzi scheme, the early investors are paid off with the contributions of many later investors, who, in turn, are paid off by the contributions of still later ones until the scheme collapses. (Paulos, 96)

In the church, we tend to arrange personal advantages that eventually result in a great cost to others. It will soon become clear that our preoccupation with the short term is not just a philosophical matter. **In the United Methodist Connection, long term is frequently the preferred orientation.** A confessional examination of this spiritual pollutant leads to the following comments:

- •We fail to make the forward looking decision in the church because we fear the reaction of others. Then we miss an opportunity to expand our ministry and our church needlessly falters. But, do you not see? We must be realistic.
- •We fail to offer forgiveness and reconciliation to someone. Suddenly, the opportunity is gone and both of our lives are pained and limited. We both spend future years trying to compensate for that early wound. But, do you not see? It was never really convenient for us. And more, it was the other person's responsibility to take the initiative.
- •We fail to save time for study and prayer. Then life presents us with an opportunity and all we have to offer are immature faith and values, an uncritical reflection of our culture. But, do you not see? There is so much to do and we are always so tired.
- •We use resources caring for institutional maintenance here at home and do not contribute all our missions askings. It is a great temptation and one encouraged by good people. Then we finally remember that apportionments always touch the lives of real people. The absence of these gifts results in genuine pain. But, do you not see? We do not know their names and will never see them. For that reason, the matter does not seem very urgent to us.

The Master once asked what we could possibly gain if we built new barns and fearfully hoarded. When life is finally over and evaluated, it will be too late to claim the wisdom that only life given away in service has value. Such a struggle! It is so hard to maintain the balance between important, immediate concerns, and the long term vision. Please, God, help us for this balance is what will liberate us to be a missionary people.

The Dread Enemy

What is the source of all this spiritual pollution? What follows is a troubling thought. We are aware that words placed in the right combination carry extraordinary power. Just two simple words standing side-by-side are enough to create memories, deep feelings, and long reflection. For instance, consider the two words "dread enemy."

Many years ago, I developed the habit of reading each day the psalm of my year. When I was forty-five years old, I read Psalm 45 each day. The next year, I read each day Psalm 46. Not long ago, it was time to read Psalm 64: "Hear my voice, O God, in my complaint; preserve my life from the dread enemy."

For seven months, I pondered these words. Over and again, I wondered, "Who or what is the dread enemy?" The psalm replied: Those who make "secret plots," who scheme, "who aim bitter words," who are persistent in secret plots, believing that no one will see them, whose tongue is their weapon, a tongue that will cause God to wound them.

One day, with great caution, I wrote in my journal the names of two or three persons whose behavior seemed to fit the description. I had witnessed their cynicism nibble away at the strength of the church. I had seen good people scarred for life by the attitude and behavior of these persons. Immediately I scribbled in my journal: *Oh, be careful! How easy to give these persons more influence than they deserve by dwelling upon their presence. Easier yet to be paranoid and see signs of this behavior where it does not exist.*

Then came a second reflection. Psalm 64 suggests secret plots that no one can see. Normally what is said or done is quickly known by many persons. "Who can see us?" The answer: "Usually many people can and will delight in telling what they know." Those who repeat the so-called secret information, without intending to do so, add to the painfulness of the original plot.

Now a third and most troubling reflection. Perhaps, just perhaps, I am my own dread enemy. Is it possible that unhealed memories, cherished prejudices or self-destructive behavior are an erosive acid corroding my own soul? Or again, are my caustic behavior and sharp-edged tongue harming me as much as I am harming others? From this perspective, the expression "dread enemy" sounds even more appalling. My last journal entry for that day was, *Oh, God, preserve my life from myself.*

A final reflection. How will we come to terms with the source of spiritual pollution? The wisdom of our spiritual ancestors is so helpful here. We must pray to God if we genuinely want the preservation of our lives. Only God, through Jesus Christ, can give us the healing of our memories, the strength to persevere in time of affliction, the capacity to offer forgiveness to those who despitefully use us, and the maturity to amend certain harmful aspects of our behavior. In helping us to cope with the dread enemy, God can also help us avoid being a dread enemy for someone else.

Order of the Crutch

Dr. Martin Marty, Lutheran theologian and historian, has said, "God rides the lame horse and carves the rotten wood." Even this short discussion of spiritual pollution should be enough to prompt us to agree. This survey of troublesome pollutants is in no way exhaustive. Most of us could go on adding to the list. However, the suggestions here may be enough to remind us that we are eligible for membership in the Order of the Crutch.

During a recent Bible study this question was asked: "When you hear the word 'lame,' what picture or symbol comes to mind?" The group made several suggestions. The one that stuck was: "A crutch." Such a curious question. It makes sense when you know that the group was studying Micah 4:

> In that day, says the LORD,
> I will assemble the lame
> and gather those who have been driven away,
>   and those whom I have afflicted.
> The lame I will make the remnant,
>   and those who were cast off, a strong nation;
> and the LORD will reign over them in Mount Zion
>   now and forevermore.   **(Micah 4:6-7)**

In the group, each of us found that we identified personally with the title, "lame." Most persons seeking to participate in the transition toward a mission identity for themselves and the church would also claim that title. In our study group, none of us struggled with severe physical limitation, except the aches and pains that come with getting older. Still, on that day, the title seemed quite personal. It still does.

SPIRITUALLY LAME: This is at the same time easiest to confess and the most dangerous. Cynical about spiritual disciplines, we avoid what generations have known about being open to God's presence. Put off by religious styles offensive to us, we turn away from any form of genuine faith development. Offended by our early religious training, we do not want anyone to offer us suggestions or make invitations. Compulsive about our schedule and perceived pressures, we are either too distracted or too tired to have time for study and prayer. Skeptical about the failures of the church, we doubt that organized religion can be helpful.

MORALLY LAME: This is the most difficult to confess and is very seductive. The culture no longer encourages high moral behavior and whispers excuses to us if we think of none for ourselves. It is not "cool" to insist on honesty, compassion, forgiveness, or a passion for justice for all persons. The excessive individualism of our time narrows our focus and prevents us from seeing the consequences of our choice on others. Our lies, unbridled anger, or violent tendencies keep building walls between us and God. As time passes, we become blind to the meaning of those walls.

MENTALLY LAME: This seems hardly worth confessing and is the breeding ground of superficial or empty faith. Our uncritical belief that learning is only for children dooms us to a religiously stunted life. We fixate at the fifth grade level and are unable to address modern complexity with the resources of Christianity. Choosing not to study or engage in challenging discussion, we are vulnerable to distortion or false teaching. This is why the central command of Christianity includes the admonition to love God with our minds. We will be held responsible for what we do not know and refuse to learn.

Many of us may be aware that our name is on the membership roll of the Order of the Crutch. In The United Methodist Church, we call acknowledgment of our membership in this Order "repentance." We are aware that admitting our membership is a most appropriate action if we want to open ourselves to Christ's loving grace and forgiveness. This admission is the gateway to the full richness of the Christian life.

Our prayer may be: "I am not perfect, O God. With my best effort, I continue to fail. I am so lame! Please help me, forgive me!" In Micah we hear words of wonderful assurance. God claims the lame, the castoffs, as God's own special people. God loves persons just like us. We become the seedbed out of which will grow the reign of God!

Someone suggested that we should call for an annual reunion of the Order of the Crutch. A proper response might be: "We already do that." Every week, once a year, and once every four years we gather, we members of the Order, to "ask the Lord's blessing."

Hungry and restless, aware of the profound change that has already taken place and continues to take place, Christian pilgrims seek to live through a period of transition by exploring the Christian disciplines and dealing with spiritual pollution. It is only by following such pathways that we can now turn our attention to our hunger for congregations that draw us into the mission of Jesus Christ. We are in an era of discovery and being discovered.

CHAPTER FIVE

Something Seems to Draw You: Congregations Electric with God's Spirit

To understand the current situation among our congregations, we must introduce the word "illusion." According to the Random House *Webster's College Dictionary*, an illusion is "something that deceives by producing a false or misleading impression of reality; a perception that represents what is perceived in a way different from the way it is in reality." It is normal for a person to live with a few illusions. Although we are in error, we perceive a situation in a particular way, believe that what we perceive is reality, and organize our lives around either half-truth or falsehood. As long as we do not hold too many illusions we can usually manage life with reasonable productivity and minimum harm. However, when we perceive the essential parts of our life in error and act on that error, we are capable of doing great harm. Further, failing to grasp the true nature of the situation, we deny ourselves opportunity to be at our best.

Why another excursion through the dictionary? Because too many congregations are planning their entire life around an illusory view of their context for ministry. *Christendom is dead!* In Christendom the culture created a favorable climate for the church. The church's language, music, and teachings were acceptable enough to allow effective communication. People were interested in the church and would frequently participate without being invited.

Christendom is dead! Large portions of the population find little value in the activity of our congregations. Our music is not their music. Our normal faith language holds few connecting points for them. Much of our program and mission does not touch their life. It would not occur to many that they could find help in our congregations for their spiritual yearnings. Worst of all, many find such a disjuncture between what we advocate and how we live that they are either offended by us or discount our credibility. In the new culture, most people are not angry with the church. They are indifferent.

Many congregations live with the assumption that this is not true. They still look at their culture, the context for their ministry, and assume that it is the same now as it has always been. Based on that illusion, they fashion their worship services, educational experiences, and forms of communication in a style that few outsiders understand. Someone may object that some congregations plan in this manner and still grow. In a few instances, they grow rapidly. That phenomenon is simple testimony to how many people in the population still live with the same illusion.

"If it ain't broke, don't fix it." This has become a creedal statement in many discussions. Everything is fine as it is. Give us a little more enthusiasm. Let our pastor work a little harder. Concentrate on the local situation and keep the larger church off our backs. Then things will get better. That creedal statement is a vote for the status quo. It ignores the real question: "How can we improve our approach to ministry so our purpose, our mission, will be better fulfilled? How can we better serve God and the world

God loves? Is there any way we can effectively reach those persons who are not now and perhaps have never been a part of the Christian faith?"

Christendom is dead! Congregations that want to be centers of faith development and genuine mission outreach must now claim their identity as missionary congregations with missionary leaders. The time for sensitive listening and observation, for thoughtful innovation and experimentation, is upon us. Churches claiming this new identity will live with maximum ambiguity and frustration. The way forward is not clear. The new pathways must be found. In a recent article, Martin Marty put the matter well when he said:

When its leaders and visionaries have an eye on the future, a trace of chaos in the soul, and a regard for the innovative in venerable scriptures and traditions, organized religion can be an agent of change, rich in potential too seldom now realized. (Martin Marty, "The Disorganization of Organized Religion," *Illinois Issues*, Dec. 1994)

Larger numbers of servant leaders in the church are becoming aware of how harmful these crippling illusions can be. They sense the great spiritual hungers of our time and are increasingly aware that our congregations are less helpful than they might be. They are beginning to sense rigid institutionalization of the church, its organizational habits and resource expenditures, as misplaced activity and commitment. Rather than being defensive, these servant leaders are discovering God's delightful "gift of incompleteness." There is a dynamic process in creation. God's spirit is still active, bringing into being the coming reign of God. We United Methodists acknowledge this dynamic with our language about "going on to perfection." Each generation of the church is invited by God to participate in the continuing creative process that instills the church and its congregations with vitality and hope. God's invitation draws us into the future as we search for ways our congregations can be electric with God's spirit.

The Secular Context

Early in this discussion, we necessarily must come to terms with the context for ministry and mission. In a time when some religious leaders decry the secular nature of the world culture as an evil from which we must distance ourselves, missionary leaders must pause to reflect. If our task is to explore the outreach of the Christian faith, our witness to the gospel's meaningfulness to real life, then it is necessary that we understand the multiformed nature of secularization. If we do not, we will be tempted to narrow our category of thought and limit the effectiveness of our Christian witness. We are required to recognize this secular world as the world loved by God, as the arena for our mission and ministry. For us, no other world exists than the one of this moment. If we are to love life as God loves it, then we are compelled to understand it. The process of secularization takes several forms. If we study this differentiation, we might be helped as we seek to form our church for its mission of witness and outreach in this new time.

FORM ONE: This form of secularization must be seen as a faith position, a self-chosen one, the choice of a person, culture, or subculture. It represents the assertion that there is no point of transcendence within reality. Language about the existence of a divine being, a personal God who is active in and affecting the world, is seen as nonsense language. That is, the language does not correspond to anything that can be proved as real.

Why speak of this as self-definition? The Christian would contend that the definition itself does not correspond to reality. A basic flaw in the proposition is that life is, at any point, void of God's presence. Thus, the Christian will argue that all of life is sacred. One is at liberty to deny this. Such a denial has specific consequences for life. However, this denial, the claim that one is living in a secular world, is a willfully chosen faith statement. One is not required to reach this conclusion.

Some persons do arrive at this conclusion through honest intellectual processes. Their analysis of life and language raises problems and doubts too profound for them to ignore. The religious teachers they know seem unable to understand or to help. As a consequence, the most useful solution for these persons is to compartmentalize religion and its claims into a special field for unique inquiry like a separate chapter in the book, a distinct department in the university, or a subject matter available for study by interested students but not a subject that must take the time and attention of the remainder of life.

Other persons come to this conclusion through their observation of religious institutions. They see these institutions claim to represent religious beliefs, and then observe them repeatedly fail to identify with the suffering of the poor and needy. Disillusioned by institutional representatives and their proclamations concerning a loving God, these persons turn away from any acceptance of religious claims as relevant to life.

FORM TWO: A second form of secularization is observed in persons who do not deny the existence of a deity, but who live their lives without any reference to such a reality or related religious teachings. They give affirmative answers to religious polls about being religious and about belief in God. However, they unconsciously assume that if such a being as God exists, this existence has no pragmatic implication for human life. Common courtesy makes such persons hospitable to religious institutions and persons. But they insist that they not be inconvenienced or oppressed by such "religious presence." Common sense, they claim, causes them to live life without any conscious reference to any being that might be called "God."

FORM THREE: The third form of secularization is that of the abused and mistreated: victims of injustice and cruelty, victims of poverty and political oppression, and victims of violence and neglect. Such persons are frequently secular in the sense that they reject the claims of religious institutions. Violence against their person, their sense of well-being, frequently by the institution of religion or its representatives, estrange these persons from all religious claims. This form of secularization is most dramatically seen in persons who are sexually abused. When this abuse is by representatives of the church, the resulting profound alienation produces the despair of a deeply secularized personality.

FORM FOUR: The "religiously secular" is the final form to be explored. These are persons in the Christian church who use the words of faith, sometimes in a way that seems violent and angry, but who act and make choices without any apparent acceptance of the presence of God in life or the validity of Christian teachings. They use religion to achieve their political ends. They easily violate truth, respect for persons, or concern for integrity when such violations are convenient to the support of their chosen ideology. Within this form of secularization, religious faith is limited to religious words.

Such a differentiation of secular form or expression helps one to identify the challenges that face the church's ministry and mission in the future. Each form of secularization requires a distinct form of witness. Oversimplification of the nature of secularity weakens our ability to be contagious in our expression of the Christian faith.

Are We Contagious?

I can remember in my youth seeing "Quarantined" signs tacked on the front door of a neighbor's house. Our family never had that sign on our house. There was an annual event, however, when I was declared "contagious" by my mother and restricted to house and bed. From the first through eighth grade, I had an annual case of the measles: "German measles," "hard measles," and "three-day measles" several times. My mother became an expert on spotting measles.

Following the theory that the sooner I broke out the less sick I would be, Mother would place me immediately in a hot tub for a soak. That promoted the breaking out, as I recall. Since I stayed in the tub until there were results, I also looked a bit like a prune. When I had passed the "breaking out" test, it was to bed with the shades pulled to protect my eyes. Measles was serious in those days, so I suppose all those precautions made sense. From my perspective, it meant being stuck in the house while things far more interesting were going on outside. My vigorous protest always produced the same answer: "You are contagious! You will be until the measles go away." A tough sentence, especially when I could hear the gang outside deliberately enjoying themselves in our front yard, even asking to borrow my football!

Such memories can prompt one to ponder. Are there any contagious churches? Perhaps the more pointed question is: "What do people catch from us when they associate with us?" Every congregation casts a shadow that touches the lives of persons around it. For good or ill, each person so touched is somehow changed.

Are our hope and our confidence in God contagious?

One of our challenges is to form congregations whose spirit, hospitality, worship, and small group life will help turn people's fixed attention from anxiety and despair to confidence that God can be trusted. When persons are near us, we pray they will gain from us assurance that God's way can be found and followed while we live at the very heart of life's struggle.

In our congregation, is it our faith, our trust in God that is contagious?

At a dinner for a retiring Lutheran bishop, one speaker remarked that to be around him was automatically to think of the words "sincerity" and "faith." Although I had known this bishop for only a short time, I found this comment most appropriate. He trusted God and I knew that he did. Without being fully aware of it, I found myself trusting because of his quiet faith. The missionary congregation yearns to have such an influence. When persons participate in our congregational life, we pray that their faith is stronger because they sense that we are on a faith pilgrimage. We seek forgiveness when they catch from us the "Henny Penny" complex, the hopeless cry that the "sky is falling" and everything is falling apart.

Is the joy in our congregations contagious?

We dream of congregations where persons are drawn to the gospel because they find warmth and hospitality. We want people to know they are welcome and wanted. What a delight if the ambiance of our gatherings is playful, happy, perhaps even joyful!

Do our congregations have a contagious sense of ministry, an attractive commitment to participate in God's loving service in this world?

A congregation whose primary concern is service in God's name is exciting! Such congregations have an energy and purpose that make them attractive and attracting. The congregation's vocational commitment is contagious. Participation in such congregations subtly draws persons into fresh commitment. They see members as Christian stewards, quietly and naturally going about a calling to service.

One thing I know! Maturing Christians in a missionary congregation are contagious. They demonstrate a trust in God, a brightness and playfulness in joy, and a quiet but powerful stewardship that must never be quarantined. The missionary congregation is populated with ordinary Christian people whose calling is not to offset the chilling influence of the cynic, the quarrelsomeness, or hopelessness. More!

Much more! We are invited by God to be the pillars of the family of God, the ones who remind others of whose we are and who we are called to be. Such is an authentic congregation.

Marks of an Authentic Church

"Whose hammer is this? Does anyone know who borrowed my saw? Anyone seen my screwdriver?" If you have taken part in a congregational work day or a Volunteers in Mission program, you will immediately recognize these questions. People work out of one another's toolboxes. At the end of the day you hope you can find all the tools you brought with you. For that reason, many years ago I developed the habit of putting my private mark on each of my tools. That mark establishes their identity.

In this day of transition when there is confusion over what constitutes authenticity in congregations, are there "marks" that identify a Christian congregation living toward the future? If people come to one of our congregations, what do they have a right to expect?

"Is one of the marks congregational growth? Doesn't that count?"

Yes, of course! We expect that our witness and ministry will draw people into participation. However, a congregation can grow quite rapidly and still not be authentic. The test question is, "What happens to people when they participate in our congregations?"

"Is one of the marks of authenticity a strong financial program? Should we be concerned about financial stewardship?"

You speak the truth! Financial stewardship is necessary for the spiritual health of each Christian and for a strong mission outreach in the church. However, a congregation can have ample funds and still be turned in on itself. The test question is: "How is the money used?"

What follows is a trial list of identifying marks. As we seek to live our way into the future, the invitation is to improve upon this list.

1. An authentic church constantly improves a faith development program for those who participate in its life, helping them to grow in their understanding of the Christian faith, the Scripture, and the United Methodist heritage. This congregation focuses on helping participants be faithful disciples.

2. An authentic church offers a variety of worship experiences in recognition that persons vary greatly in their response to worship. In addition to meeting the worship needs of the current participants, this congregation listens carefully to its community in order to discover what forms of worship will be genuinely helpful to others and draw them into participation.

3. An authentic church ministers to persons in the surrounding community. Its members are sensitive to local needs, persons in trouble, unjust situations, and to social conditions that are harmful to persons or the environment. God has placed our congregations in specific communities. What is it that God needs from the congregation in each place?

4. An authentic church is constantly alert for ways to join in ministry with nearby congregations so as to make more effective its efforts to meet needs. Joint efforts with other United Methodist congregations and with ecumenical coalitions are normal to these congregations. The authentic congregation has such a passion for faith-sharing and mission service that there is little room for competitiveness.

5. An authentic church understands that the care of God's creation is part of Christian stewardship and seeks ways to express that care in its own practices. It models for the community respect for God's creation and joins with others as an advocate for ecological responsibility in business and government.

6. An authentic church sees "the world as its parish." For that reason, its people study the mission needs of the global community and actively share in meeting those needs through the church's mission program. In addition to World Service budget contributions, the authentic congregation takes on numerous capital Advance Special projects. The constant effort of the congregation is to help its members be sensitive to service opportunities in the name of Jesus Christ.

This list is incomplete. It is offered with confidence but also with an invitation. This would be an opportune moment to stop reading and begin your own list of the identifying marks of an authentic church seeking to be in mission in a new day.

Upon What Shall These Congregations Depend?

A structural engineer hurried through my office door. His first words were: "We must allow no one else to enter the sanctuary under any circumstances!" The congregation was building a new educational wing and we also wanted to consider remodeling the sanctuary. The engineer was studying the strength of this old building. He had borrowed a ladder and climbed into the rafters. After a few minutes, he hurried back down with an ashen face, shocked by his discovery. This is what he had found:

The sanctuary contained, as decorative items, four false columns on each side wall, with a small decorative cap at the top of each. The columns appeared to hold up the ceiling. In fact, they were nothing more than two-by-fours covered with plaster. Over the years, the brick walls of this old church building had bulged out on each side, allowing the ceiling to settle down on top of the decorative columns. All that was keeping the ceiling off the heads of our worshiping congregation were a few two-by-fours, decorative coping, and seventy-five-year-old plaster.

Such a useful parable! We can be as startled as that engineer with the discovery of how much we depend on false columns to support our congregations—false columns that will collapse at any point when the pressures become too great. One way to discover these illusory points of support is to listen to conversations and watch reactions in the congregation. Congregations reveal their dependency in times of pressure, in the facing or avoiding of critical issues, in experiences of conflict or confusion. Sensitive observation is an excellent early step for persons who care to live beyond the illusions.

Upon what do our congregations depend? Perhaps a point of contrast will bring the answer into clarity.

A basic emphasis of The United Methodist Church is called "Christian assurance." Such assurance is a trust, a deep form of knowing, that we are forgiven and loved by God as known in Jesus Christ. The congregation, indeed all human beings have an amazing resilience when under-girded by the confidence that Christ's love will always be theirs, will never be denied them, and will only be absent when they choose to reject it.

Mary McCleod Bethune, a remarkable African American Methodist woman, once said in a commencement address: **"Walk bravely in the light. Faith ought not to be a puny thing. If you believe, believe like a giant. And may God grant you not peace but glory."**

A Taste for Risk and Adventure

As a congregation gains assurance about the depend-ability of God's love, the sense of adventure and willingness to take risks, when seasoned by wisdom and pointed to-ward worthy goals, can be an asset of great value. Far too often the mission of Jesus Christ falters because honorable Christian people are unwilling to put themselves at risk for a higher cause.

Not all risk-taking is mature. Some of it is foolishness. Here is a recent experience. Both lanes of the one-way street were packed with evening traffic, traveling at thirty-five miles per hour bumper-to-bumper. The first boy to cross the street was laughing and running as fast as he could out of a parking lot, across the sidewalk, directly in front of the automobiles and on across the second lane. I slammed on the brakes, throwing my car into a sideways slide. My relief was a mixture of gratitude that I had not hit the boy and that other cars had not hit me. As soon as traffic started to move again, another boy dashed across the street, followed by a girl, followed by another boy. They were all laughing and deliberately looking away from the automobiles so as to ignore them. That no one was killed is testimony to the fast reaction time of seasoned drivers. It was obviously a game! Who was brave enough to run into the middle of fast-moving traffic without looking at the automobiles? Who could make it all the way across both lanes of traffic? Who was chicken and who wasn't?

The entire game was possible because of the basic assumption among adolescents that nothing serious will happen to them. No matter how crazy or wild the action, they are invincible. They will never die. That day I drove away from the town heading toward home with these reflections in my mind:

1. Write it down as a miracle when a teenager reaches adulthood. That was true in my generation. In the late 1950s at a two-point charge where I was pastor, the thrill of the evening was for kids to lie in the middle of the highway and see if the cars would miss them. A teenager reaching adulthood today is even more of a miracle. Today's youth are at risk. Every congregation needs a few adults who love kids, are trusted by them, and are wise enough to help them dream great dreams.

2. The youthful assumption of invincibility is one of the reasons privates are young and generals are old. In a war, persons actually doing the fighting need to believe that the risks are not real. They need to believe that war is a grand adventure where everyone is a hero. People only die in the movies. It will never happen to them or their friends.

3. This brings us back to the congregation called upon by God to risk an adventure for the benefit of future mis-

sion. Running between automobiles as a game is stupid. Putting the cause of Jesus Christ above survival is mature discipleship.

4. The modern church is not endangered by challenging proposals and risk-taking leaders. Failures that threaten our congregations originate in such phrases as: "What's in it for me?" "We need to take care of our own needs, then see what is left over." "Don't tell me about sacrifice. This is a new day. People don't think that way anymore!" "I can remember back when. . . ."

I certainly hope none of those kids were injured or killed that day. What a tragic waste that would be. Perhaps they will live long enough to express more constructive risk-taking in one of our congregations. Perhaps wisdom will replace recklessness, and they will learn to risk in the name of a higher cause. Perhaps that higher cause will be found in the will of God. When those youth are old enough to begin to pick up the reins of leadership in our congregations, we will still be in transition, in search for the congregations of the future. We will need their sense of adventure to show us the way.

The Gift of Sanctuary

One vision that may help us live into the future is the vision of sanctuary, the congregation as a sacred place where safety, comfort, and a sense of "home" can be discovered. It is worth pondering how our congregations can be such a place. The hunger for sanctuary is great.

"Please grant the gift of sanctuary." Those were the words of a prayer. They were my words. In uttering them I had reached back into a rich Christian tradition. If you could make it to the sanctuary, Christians would protect you and provide hospitality. In a sanctuary environment, in a way difficult to articulate, one can have a growing appreciation for the presence of God.

A short search in Hebrew Scripture will allow you to discover the requirement to establish "cities of refuge." The Israelites were commanded to establish these cities in order that people who were in danger or unjustly accused could find a place of temporary safety. If you could make your way to the gates of one of the cities of refuge, you would be immediately protected from those who were seeking to harm you and offered hospitality until the justice of the matter could be settled.

The church of the future will need to be such a place. When persons trust us and come for counseling or help, in their vulnerability they ask us for "sanctuary." Our prayer: "Please, God, transform this relationship into your sanctuary." Laity and clergy, we are all hosts in God's sanctuary. There is no place among us for indifference to those in need. Sexual or physical abuse must never be permitted to take place. Love and respect condition our words and actions. We stand with others in the face of threat. Before God, we recognize our responsibility for their safety. They have a right to expect that they are safe with us.

When persons enter our home, in their vulnerability they ask us for "sanctuary." Our prayer: "Please, God, transform this home into your sanctuary." We say, "Welcome to our home! We are pleased to see you. Come and warm yourself, join us at our table. We draw our circle of love around you. While you are here you are one of us." Hospitality, courtesy, generous sharing, protection: these are the themes of the place we call home. Before God, we are responsible to extend sanctuary to all who come to us.

When persons approach our congregations, in their vulnerability they ask us for "sanctuary." Our prayer: "Please, God, transform this congregation into your sanctuary." The congregation can be a local parish, a committee meeting, an annual conference session, a training event, a study group, or any other gathering of Christian people. There the circle of love, hospitality, courtesy, generous sharing, and protection is drawn around those who come our way. Before God, we are responsible to extend sanctuary to all persons among us. Certainly that is a reasonable expectation for the missionary congregation of the future.

Someone recently said, "Our people look upon our church building and grounds in the same way they look upon a public school or a place of business. Our church is a program center, a utilitarian building increasingly expensive to maintain. When our congregation gathers for worship or other occasions, there is no discernible difference in attitudes or relationships than when they are in other public gatherings."

Where are the storytellers? Where are the people who remember? Where are the persons who understand the meaning of sacred place, of sanctuary? Where are the persons who will take a moment in a meeting for private conversation to say, "Let me share with you what we have experienced here, what this place has meant to our people"? Who is telling the new members the history of our people in this place? Who is inviting them to share in that history? Whose sense of the sacred sanctuary serves as a model for young people so they can intuitively understand the meaning behind the memories?

We speak of critical mass here. It will not take very many persons offering sanctuary in a congregation to begin the transformation. They will be the leaven in a missionary congregation who will gradually create a place of sacred safety and peace.

The Nurturing of Leadership

Tomorrow's congregations will affirm the urgent need for strong and visionary leadership. These congregations will take responsibility for identifying such potential leaders and nurturing them into the full expression of their giftedness.

In reflecting on this responsibility, I want to say a word of appreciation for two persons who nurtured me. The first was my pastor. At an important time, Harold Criswell was my spiritual guide and skillful question raiser. He helped me clarify a call to ordained ministry. This faithful Christian, caring husband and father, effective preacher, and skillful administrator nurtured me through invitations. Martha and I were young laypersons in the congregation. We were invited to sing in the choir, a legitimate request for Martha and an act of grace for me. Before we were fully aware of it, we were helping to organize a new young adult class. In those days I had only a vague awareness of an outreach program called "Two By Two." Harold said, "Why not come to two evenings of training, David? You will find it interesting." I went and I did.

Another invitation: "I will be doing some calling on people in the neighborhood. Would you like to come along with me?" I went. Then came an invitation to serve on the Official Board. The church basement needed to be painted. How would I like to help? Although I was now traveling several days a week in my job, it seemed natural to say, "Yes." Callers were needed for the stewardship campaign. My parents had always done this so I replied: "Yes, I guess so." Then I was to read scripture in the worship service. "I will try, if you will help me." Of course he would help me. I came on Saturday evening to the sanctuary and we practiced until I felt comfortable. My pastor expanded my experience and confidence through a series of invitations. He taught me by example and tutoring. He never left me so much on my own that I would be discouraged by failure.

The second person was my first district superintendent. From the beginning, Charles Tyler continually expanded opportunities for leadership responsibilities: service on district committees, secretary for the District Board of Ordained Ministry, dean of church camps, and leader of workshops. When the time was right, his nomination placed me to conference responsibilities. He was always in contact so that I never felt abandoned. He expanded my experience in the pattern that kept me learning and gaining confidence. In the mission congregations of the future, laypersons and pastors will have it within their power to invite others into expanding realms of leadership in the church and beyond. The power of the invitation, enhanced by tutoring and encouragement, will release spiritual capacity in remarkable ways. In the process, the ministry of the church increases and expands. Servant leaders living into that tomorrow may find some of these ideas worth pondering:

1. Ministry of encouragement: One of the greatest compliments a person can receive is, "You always encouraged other persons, especially the young ones and new people." Encouragement can be as simple as "Thank you!" The **encourager** not only steps aside to make room for new leaders but cheers them on.

2. Power of gradually expanding leadership opportunities: Assess the past experience and skill level of others. Invite them to experiences and responsibilities that will challenge but not overwhelm them. Too frequently we see promising persons and immediately place them in positions beyond their readiness. They either fail or struggle just short of a satisfying success. Discouragement and burn out frequently result.

3. Christian formation experiences that encourage maturity in faith: Potential new leaders in the church need small-group and class-meeting types of experiences that help them grapple with issues of the Christian faith. Tomorrow's church needs well-grounded leaders, persons who can base their leadership in the vision and wisdom of the Christian faith. The current church can receive no more severe criticism than that the faith development opportunities we now provide were not effective. There is a hunger to study the Bible, to examine the beliefs of our church, and to struggle with life issues.

4. Leadership seminars: Tomorrow's congregation will create leadership development seminars for thoughtfully recruited persons. In every congregation there are persons not yet in leadership who could be strong leaders in the future. The pastor and lay leaders search for these persons. They are candidates for a multiple-week seminar. These seminars can include sessions on the mission of the church, the theological basis for leadership in the church, basic leadership skills and organizational dynamics, and a vision for how the church of the future can live out its calling of faith development and mission outreach. In congregations of limited membership, clusters of churches can offer these seminars. Leaders developed in this context will be a gift to both church and community.

Pathways of Graceful Return

An appropriate amount of our attention and energy is focused on reaching persons who have not been a part of the Christian faith, who have never participated in the life of a congregation. We try to focus on the "population at a distance." We examine our congregational life, our worship style, our hospitality, and the effectiveness of our ministry in order to offer hospitality and welcome to those we have not been able to reach in the past. However, there is another group of persons who are part of the "population at a distance." They are the ones who left the church some time ago and carried with them a spiritual yearning so basic that it will not die.

It is so hard to return to the church!

Some have simply been neglectful, wandered away, and got distracted. Now it is embarrassing to return. Some left in anger, offended in a relationship or bruised by some event. Now they are not sure how to save face while they try to return. Others felt that they were treated unjustly and are having a difficult time forgiving some of the persons they know they must meet if they return to the sanctuary.

Yet others dropped out for a while and were never contacted by anyone inviting them back. Perhaps worst of all,
a few have tried to return after a long absence only to
realize that no one seems to realize they were gone.

The roster has not been completed until we remember one
more such group. They left because the experience in our
congregation was without meaning. Like that large group who
have never responded, these are persons who have not found
participation in our congregational life of any significance.
For some our worship was dull. For others, sermons and
Sunday school classes did not seem relevant to the reality of
their world. For others, the church did not provide meaningful ways to make a positive difference in the world. They
stayed away for a while and discovered they had lost all
motivation to return. Indeed, the idea of returning only oc-
curs to them in moments of unusual need.

How blessed is that congregation that creates a "path-
way of graceful return." Blessed is the congregation that
provides a careful balance of warm welcome and uncrowd-
ed space, which offers a genuine greeting without smoth-
ering the persons with excessive attention or the demand
for explanation.

The graceful return is encouraged when persons who
miss worship are contacted with a phone call after the
second Sunday and a personal visit after the third Sunday.
These contacts are a simple message that the person was
missed and given a specific invitation to participate in a
congregational activity.

The graceful return is made easier when a congregation is trained to extend respectful and warm welcomes to
one another wherever they meet, in sanctuary, shopping
center, or community event.

The graceful return seems genuine when the congregation contacts inactive members not to ask the reason for
their absence, but to request suggestions about how the

activities of the congregation might be more helpful and interesting.

The graceful return seems worth risking when the congregation constantly improves its worship and spiritual growth opportunities and when persons are requested to participate through direct and personal invitations. Invite persons by telephone, personally addressed direct mail, and face-to-face invitations. These signal that each person is wanted and valued.

The graceful return has spiritual integrity when leaders in the congregation regularly pray for each member, especially those persons who are currently inactive. Although never publicly mentioned, the spirit created by such authentic concern is obvious in even the largest congregation.

With such a graceful spirit **the missionary congregation** seeks to be invitational, seeks to make it easier for persons to return to their spiritual homes. This congregation reads with special sensitivity the New Testament words:

> And I will show you a still more excellent way . . . Love is patient; love is kind; love is not envious or boastful or arrogant or rude. It does not insist on its own way; it is not irritable or resentful; it does not rejoice in wrong, but rejoices in the truth.   (1 Corinthians 12:3*b*–13:4-6)

Laity and Clergy in Collegial Relationship

Sometimes an important truth is made dramatically obvious. A clergywoman of the Episcopal Church did that for me. She was an excellent preacher. Had one not observed her difficulty in moving to the pulpit, one would never guess she had cerebral palsy. Then came the moment when she needed to turn the page of her manuscript. It was painful to watch as she struggled. Responding to God's call, she had completed, over great self- doubt, her theological training and had been ordained.

Of course, she said, she would never be able to preach. However, her bishop had insisted that she take preaching classes. In the opening session, the professor read the story of Moses and Aaron. Her report of the professor's reading was something like this: "Moses pleaded that he was not a public speaker. It was Aaron who had that gift. God was asking the wrong person. God's reply was simple. God was fully aware that Aaron was a gifted public speaker. However, if God had wanted Aaron to do the talking, Aaron would have been called instead of Moses!"

It was hard to miss the message. Now she fulfills her vocation with a confidence born of trust in God who called her. She spoke about the ministry of persons with handicapping conditions at a national gathering in Minneapolis for persons in pastoral care and counseling. I was there to speak on the relationship of the church in appointments beyond the local church. She left me with these wonderful gifts of insight.

At one point, she referred to most of us as **"those persons temporarily physically able."** The truth of that phrase was immediately obvious to me. As she spoke I remembered the pain in my left ankle, an injury that brought my running program to a permanent finish. This new physical limitation and the resulting weight gain were irritating. In addition, I experienced a renewed back pain that made getting out of bed or a chair more difficult. When I complained about it, Martha mentioned something about "a person my age . . . ."

Serious illness, accidents, and the normal aging process create limitations for us all. How appropriate it is to thank God for each moment of good health and free movement. And, more important, how thankful we can be that God continues to draw us into ministry despite our limitations. When the handicapping conditions must be faced, this gifted young priest gave us the model. She said: **"Enough of the moaning and groaning. We are all the limited**

servants of Christ. God uses even our limitations as we fulfill our Christian calling."

She spoke of her sense of dread before the first time she was to celebrate the Eucharist.

How would she fulfill the physical movements of that great sacrament? She grew angry at her illness, angry that she could not celebrate the sacrament the way she wanted to. She was still angry as she first approached the table. Then it was that she learned!

Discussing the situation with a lay assistant, she had worked out a way to celebrate the Eucharist. The lay assistant would be her hands. As she stood before the table, she was surprised to feel a profound peace. Her learning: She could only fulfill her calling to ordained ministry as she worked in closest harmony with a layperson. Without that help her own ministry was impossible.

No matter how obvious this might seem, it is an understanding greatly needed by both clergy and laity. The vision of ministry in The United Methodist Church holds laity and clergy in a complementary and mutually supportive relationship. Both have vital functions in the ministry of the church. Ministry is weakened when either fails in responsibility. Each is stronger when supported by the other. The new church needed in our time is characterized by the affirmation and celebration of the distinct ministry of both.

In the days ahead, we will be affirming "the ministry of all Christians." The full power of our mission as disciples will be curtailed unless laity and clergy love and respect one another and affirm their distinct responsibilities. Power struggles and competition for position and privilege are alien to missionary leaders. Companionship and mutual support are the norms. This is how it will be among us.

The powerful relationship between laity and clergy is more dramatically obvious when we consider the full dimension of lay ministry. A small group of laypersons will be selected in the congregation for servant leadership.

They will teach, provide music, assist in worship, serve as spiritual leaders, and chair a few committee meetings. If we are successful, the missionary congregation will help the vast majority of laity to claim their mission to the world. These persons will prepare themselves through faith development and then transform workplace, volunteer organizations, political activity, neighborhood, and home. The congregation will be for them the community of nurture, support, and learning. The primary arena of their ministry will be in all the structures of this world so loved by God.

Preaching: A Necessary Ingredient

Do persons attend worship because a friend invited them, because of a variety of program opportunities in the congregation, because of music, or because of preaching? Researchers do not offer any consensus on this, which probably indicates all are valid. However, there is one group of researchers who agree that preaching is very important. That is the regular report of district superintendents after interviewing the Pastor-Parish Relations Committees. The negative factor determines preaching's rank order. If their pastor is considered an effective preacher, the committee will name other factors as more important. If their pastor is a poor preacher, preaching will be listed high on their list of desirable attributes for the next appointment.

The missionary pastor will need to be an effective communicator, including preaching. Lord Donald Soper in a seminar on preaching some time ago said: "Every powerful social movement in human history has been fired by oratory." In that presentation, Dr. Soper had little patience with the pastor who did not prepare and preach at the highest possible level. He insisted that any pastor could be a good preacher if he or she worked at it.

Increasing numbers of persons attending worship services have had limited exposure to mature teaching about the Christian faith. Most of what they know is at a simplistic level. Nothing in their lives has equipped them with an accurate and well-informed understanding. Add to this dynamic the realization that the worship service with its sermon is their only exposure to the faith and you have your evidence that preaching must carry a heavy load now and in the future. If Christians of the future are to be spiritually formed, much of the content of their faith will come from the sermon.

Some pastors argue that sermons that will draw people to regular participation must be very elementary, not too heavy, with use of humor and life-related stories. After the sermon draws people in, then one must try to involve them in small groups; only there is a thoughtful presentation of the gospel possible. That seems to be the experience of many successful pastors. However, the argument has an important flaw. It is an unusual congregation where the number of persons attending study/discussion groups equals worship attendance. An important number of persons find all the Christian guidance and instruction they will ever receive in the worship service, especially in the sermon.

Of even greater urgency is the nature of the preaching act. The sermon is a Word/Event. Reflecting the Word (Logos) of the Creation wherein God spoke all creation into existence, the continuing Word of the sermon is an action/event. The Spirit of God is present in that dialogical space releasing new creation. Further, in that first Word/Event of the Creation, the Word-in-action was the Christ. God in Christ, Christ in God, bringing into being all that exists. When the congregation or the pastor fails to grasp the active presence of the Christ, working with both presenter and listener, then the marvel of the moment is denied. When the preacher understands the nature of the preaching act, does not seek to control it, and comes with anticipation and wonder, the groundwork has been laid for the miracle. Now the heart knows the meaning of: "Woe to me if I do not proclaim the gospel."

The one who dares to put on the preaching mantle needs to remember the seven marks of the missionary preacher.

1. Our sermons will be faithful to the apostolic faith found in the Scripture and tradition. We will use many approaches and illustrate with life experience and learning from many fields of knowledge. Our touchstone will remain the faith passed on to us. The church does not ordain to "Word" as a license to pronounce anything less.

2. Sermons will be substantive, presented with skill and sensitive awareness. We will invite people to learn and commit to Christ's wisdom and grace. Occasional sermons will urge people to "work" with the pastor in a struggle with difficult questions.

3. The preaching event will grow out of the life of the people and of the pastor. For this reason, the pastor will be a student of life, living among the people, observing and asking questions. Pastors will read and contemplate in the search for understanding. Knowing that the life-questions are as important as answers given "before their time," the teaching preacher will not hesitate to struggle publicly and invite others to do the same.

4. The missionary preacher will seek to be accurate in both fact and scriptural story line. Most of us make occasional slips. Such is the stuff of our finiteness. A regular diet of slippage, however, signals to the church that the pastor is careless and does not value the opportunity.

5. Pastor/preacher/teachers will fulfill the study and preparation necessary to transform their preaching into sacred oratory. This means attention to grammar and word usage, creative use of imagery and parable, appreciation of the power of story and appropriate drama, and practice. Yes, practice. The sermon is a spoken event. Some opportunity must be given for the message to move from concept and paper into the verbal arena.

6. Pastor/preacher/teachers will not lose sight of the teaching moment. The redundant theme, the occasional explanation, the repetition of words or phrases, and the drawing of word pictures will gradually equip the congregation with unfolding knowledge.

7. Finally, the United Methodist pastor passes on to the congregation the spiritual heritage of our church. The stories of our people and the theological emphasis of our church contain cherished and useful wisdom. The missionary pastor is not silent here. Many parishioners know nothing of this heritage and are fascinated when they learn of it.

The Importance of Freedom of the Pulpit

In a conversation about future missionary congregations with missionary leaders, the freedom of our pulpits must be seen as a critical issue for the spiritual health of our church. Freedom of the pulpit, though never directly addressed, is implied throughout our Constitution and the provisions of *The Book of Discipline*. It is one of the direct results of our pastoral itineracy.

In conferences and retreats over the years, laypersons have shared with me their awareness of just how important this freedom is to their own spiritual health.

Freedom of the pulpit means that our pastors are authorized by the church in their ordination to preach the Word of God in congregations, searching through prayer and study for the meaning of the Scripture (*Book of Discipline*, pars. 430, 435, 439). Pastors are to be sensitive students of the history of our Christian movement and of current world situations. Pastors are to translate all they discover through preaching and teaching so that members may share in this spiritual quest and be challenged to grow in faith and relationships.

Freedom of the pulpit means that pastors will occasionally struggle with some perplexing social/ethical issue, seeking insight faithful to the Scripture and the ancient wisdom of our faith. The result is a prophetic word spoken with conviction and humility. The pulpit has been the seedbed of much of the reform and renewal in the nations of this world. We maintain this freedom of our pulpits in order that such a gospel might be available to congregations and society in our time as well.

Freedom of the pulpit means that a pastor preaching the gospel in The United Methodist Church cannot be censured or forced to leave by pressure groups or powerful individuals. The pastor serves in a congregation until appointed elsewhere by the bishop. Pastors are supervised by the bishop and cabinet. These simple facts preserve the spiritual freedom to proclaim the Word of God. In this climate of freedom, it is normal for United Methodists to listen respectfully to one another, entering into open dialogue as we seek greater wisdom. We hold pastors responsible for integrity and faithfulness in preaching. We create for them an environment of encouragement and freedom.

"But wait," you say. "Can no one hold pastors accountable for their preaching? Is there any biblical or theological content too extreme to be accepted? Can they say anything they want and not be challenged by anyone?"

No, not at all! The freedom of the United Methodist pulpit is not an unconditional freedom. It is conditioned by the covenants entered into by every United Methodist pastor. For example:

1. Each pastor covenants to hold high ministerial standards and to accept supervision, evaluation, and discipline within a covenant community (*The Book of Discipline* 1992, pars. 422,423).

2. Each pastor is responsible to support the established doctrines of the church (par. 2623.1.f). During preparation for ordination, the interview process for pastors includes extensive questions about faith, the Scripture, and United Methodist theological understandings (pars. 424 and 425).

3. Pastors are supervised by the bishop and district superintendent. Supervision is so important in our church that there are separate sections about it in both our Con-

stitution and in chapter 4 of *The Book of Discipline.* While great liberty is given to every pastor, there are supervisory provisions should the need arise.

4. The local church Pastor-Parish Relations Committee is advisory to the bishop and provides an evaluation process for the pastor designed to assist in personal and professional growth. It is in this confidential context that a pastor can receive helpful and constructive suggestions about the responses and concerns of the congregation (par. 444).

5. So important is the spiritual leadership of our pastors that continuing education is both provided for and expected (par. 445 and 446). The freedom of our pulpits is enriched by pastors who are students of the Scripture and prayer and thoughtful interpreters of the social/cultural conditions of the times.

United Methodist preaching is at its best when the congregation also takes its full responsibility. Preaching is always better when a congregation gives its support and encouragement to the pastor, including regular prayer for the next sermon. A special vitality is present when a congregation comes with expectancy and listens with open intensity.

A pastor is especially blessed when the congregation discusses a sermon, sharing connections and insights stimulated by the content and raising questions not addressed. It is exciting when an inspired pastor and people come together for worship. The potential for vast power is present.

The United Methodist Church has great confidence in its pastors. We believe that the freedom of our pulpits is essential for vital and growing faith. With provisions for accountability and specific expectations, the church trusts, however, that pastors are called by God, given the gifts and motivation needed for this holy calling, and are sufficiently inspired through prayer and study.

It is this bishop's conviction that this trust is well placed. Most of our pastors are faithful to their calling. They provide spiritual guidance and support to the par-

ishes where they are appointed. For this we all praise God!

He Walked Up the Center Aisle, Grinning

It may have been fatigue, the result of poor stewardship of time. It could just as easily have been a feeling that I had hit the limit of my ability and didn't know what to do next. I might have been overwhelmed by the unrelenting pressure experienced by most pastors. Whatever it was, it happened in my first full-time appointment following seminary.

I sat alone in the sanctuary and struggled with the awful sense that I had made a serious mistake. Perhaps I had misunderstood the meaning of God's call. Perhaps I should go back to my old employment while I could still do the work. Perhaps I was trapped. Sacrifice had been required to make it through the years of graduate school. Martha had gladly made it possible with her work and willingness to live alone on a student appointment most of the week. Could I now go to her and say it was all a mistake?

That wonderful congregation sensed that something was wrong. They were wise enough and patient enough to give me space for the struggle. Instead of distancing themselves in disappointment, they moved closer. We were invited to their homes, included in parties, asked to be their pastor at critical times. They quietly took up additional responsibilities without a word of criticism. However, their greatest act of love and encouragement took place one Sunday morning. The lay leader had privately planned an event. During the first hymn, the lay leader left his pew and started walking up the center aisle, a shy smile on his face. When he reached the lectern, the whole congregation was grinning.

"Pastor," he said, "please take a seat. We are taking over the worship service." Not knowing what else to do, I sat. The choir dedicated an anthem to their pastor. Several persons told the stories of helpful ministries of the past year. A youth representative, now a pastor himself, nervously thanked me for the Sunday evening program and the special camping trips. A recently married couple shared a few words. Someone presented some simple gifts of appreciation.

The lay leader spoke of the congregation's confidence in my leadership and assured me of their support. He also suggested God could do even more if I could make room for the leadership of the laity. Of course, we traveled to fellowship hall to share in a beautiful carry-in meal. The congregation, led by the lay leader, had declared a Celebration of Our Pastor Day. They knew I was struggling and they sent me a message of love. That was the first of several times when congregations helped me move through a valley of shadows.

These are difficult days for persons in all kinds of leadership. The climate is one of criticism, undermining, and unwillingness to cooperate. What is directed at civic and political leadership is also targeted toward pastors and church leaders. How liberating it is to receive a message of support!

Pastors are very important to congregations. It is critical that pastors offer their best, share their deep faith in Christ, and be available to people at points of need. We all recognize that no pastor is perfect. All of us struggle with shortcomings. Still, committed and hardworking pastors can be the vehicles chosen by God to bring hope and new faith to the congregation. We pray that they will be missionary pastors in a day filled with promise.

The congregation is very important to the pastor. Congregations may turn a pastor into a better preacher than the pastor thought possible. Congregations offer support and prayer, believing that God will use the pastor's service in special ways. Thank God for lay leaders and congregations who occasionally surprise their pastor with special times of encouragement, support, and signs of Christ's love.

Lay servant leaders are very important in Christ's ministry to this world. In these complex times, oversimplified

Christian platitudes frequently leave laypersons with empty hands in difficult circumstances. Complex ethical issues face everyone. Congregations are populated with talented and committed persons who care passionately about extending Christ's love into all of life. Some serve sacrificially as they share their time, personal strengths, and wealth in the outreach ministry of the church. In the church of the future, we must find ways and days wherein we can celebrate the faithful discipleship of all our people.

In Search of the Perfect Christmas Tree

What follows is a playful reflection on the nature of the missionary congregation of the future. The story has become one that our family tells about itself each time we discuss "this year's tree." The reflections on the story are something I wrote in my journal. This story is included here as an appreciation to those very special persons, our family, whom I love and from whom I gain hope.

The Lawson tribe was home for Thanksgiving. We drove to a nearby tree farm to select and cut the family Christmas tree. Of course, that means finding the perfect tree. There was a carload of opinions about what constitutes the perfect tree, and there were acres upon acres of trees to choose from. No problem. Keep looking. The next group of trees hides perfection.

You should have heard the chatter. "This is it! This is the best tree we've seen. . . . No, let's go over this next hill. I think I saw some fuller ones there. Just remember where this one is and we will come back and compare them. . . . Hey, everybody, come over here. I think I've found it!. . . . Oh no, look at the crooked trunk. And only the side you're on looks good."

We saw trees beautiful on one side and almost nonexistent on the other, or trees just right with trunks too big to fit in any tree stand. One tree was sprayed green and you didn't know it was dead until you put a hand on it and the needles fell like rain. Then there was the absolutely right tree all agreed upon. It turned out to be two trees growing so close they looked like one.

As we arrived at the tree farm, Martha had pointed to a tree barely inside the gate and suggested it was just right. However, the rest of us protested that you didn't settle on a Christmas tree without looking over the choices. Whoever heard of picking the tree without leaving the car! Over an hour later someone remembered Martha's tree and reluctantly agreed it was the best one we had seen. I say "reluctantly" for who would want to give the Mother of the family that story to tell for the rest of our lives?

Later remembering our family walking through the tree farm laughing and joking, I wrote the following in my journal: *Our family is a field of potentially perfect Christmas trees. Any one of us is the absolutely right one when we are at home surrounded with love, laughter, and the joy of Christmas. In that warm light, you don't even have to decorate us very much. That's why being together at Christmas is so important. We warm one another with love. We love one another regardless of a few imperfections. We gain comfort and perhaps a little beauty for the days ahead.*

That field of trees is also a bit like a United Methodist congregation. We look better from a distance. Some of us didn't manage to grow very straight. Some of us have limbs in the strangest places. There are some thick trunks without very much green above. And some of us must stand very close together just to make one whole tree. It's not perfection we can offer. We can share laughter, love, and the joy of knowing that Christ has come indeed! And we can give others the assurance that a field of less than perfect trees is prized by God!

CHAPTER SIX

Connections That Help: Hands and Hearts in Mutual Support

Is the Denomination Still Important?

As a point of entry? Here the importance is limited. For more than twenty years working pastors have been aware that denominational loyalty is a limited motivation for persons choosing a congregation. In small towns and open country situations where there is a limited number of churches, the choice is usually between "mainline" and "evangelical community." Yet even here the strength of services and programs offered will tend to overcome such basic orientation. Rural culture is well urbanized. Levels of education compare well with that of cities. Rural families normally drive considerable distances for business and shopping. Their willingness to drive a distance to a desirable church is limited only by family ties.

In medium-sized and larger congregations located in county seat towns and cities, people tend to look for congregations that they perceive will meet their needs. They look for hospitality, an informal ambience, good music, an interesting sermon, lively worship, a strong youth and children's program, and a schedule of events that supports freedom for family and recreational plans. The conservative cohort of the population will sometimes respond to a "high demand" congregation. Most of the population is soon put off by such demands and will look for congregations that are more invitational and need oriented.

This does not suggest that no one remains loyal to her or his denominational family. Even young adults in impressive numbers look for "their church." Some pastors and congregational leaders fail to honor this loyalty. Made insensitive by a few church growth books and church consultants, these leaders express their disdain for denominational affiliation, believing that they must do so to attract new participants. In the process they alienate persons by undervaluing their commitment and making them feel unwanted. The missionary congregation has a hospitality that makes room for and provides for great diversity, honoring and respecting each person in his or her search for faith formation and committed service.

Nurturing and mission-sending functions. Here the denominational family becomes very important. Once persons become part of The United Methodist Church, they have a right to know about its faith heritage and its outreach ministries. This will be the church in whose tradition they will experience their faith formation. We do not claim our tradition to be best or the only valuable one. That would be inappropriate arrogance. We do claim that our tradition is an honorable one born out of the faith struggles of impressive spiritual ancestors. It is an environment in which persons can grow in relationship with God. We cheat new members when we fail either to inform them about this church or to teach them of its values. To invite persons to join our church and affirm our membership vows but withhold from them a thoughtful awareness of our nature is dishonest.

It will also be through The United Methodist Church that these new participants will be invited to share their faith in action. This church will help them identify channels of service and facilitate their participation. Through our communication network they will learn of our global mission outreach and will hear the stories of what they and others are doing together to share the faith and express compassion. They will discover how the close connection in The United Methodist Church coordinates our efforts so we can join hands and hearts in common service, thereby amplifying our impact. Again, to hide this powerful means of mission involvement is not only dishonest but is also to influence negatively their spiritual development. When faith is channeled into compassionate service we discover the fire of faith.

Origin of United Methodist Conferences

The place was London. The opening day was Monday, June 25, 1744. The Right Reverend John Wesley had sent letters to several clergy and lay assistants, inviting them to meet to give advice "respecting the best methods of carrying on the work of God." The originating purpose of the conference was "to aid in preserving unity, to encourage those who most suffered from mobs and social ostracism, to maintain the organization of the societies, and to allow for the systematic transferring of the pastors from one point to another."

Planning the agenda for that first conference was simple. First they adopted resolutions for the governance of the conference. Then followed a lengthy and intense season of prayer. Conferencing together, those attending spent five days discussing two fundamental questions.

1. "What to teach?" They knew theirs was a spiritual movement. The content of their teaching and preaching needed to be focused. Facing a great spiritual void, Wesley insisted they needed to stand together as they presented a message of depth and passion. The gospel was to be at the center of all they taught and did.

2. "What to do?" or, **"How to regulate the doctrine, discipline, and practice of the ministry and the society"** (James M. Buckley, *Constitutional and Parliamentary History of the Methodist Episcopal Church* [New York: Eaton & Mains, 1912; Cincinnati: Jennings & Graham, 1912]). In this portion of the conference, the covenants of discipline were first defined. Their covenant with one another would include specific spiritual disciplines and life practices. Having made such covenant with one another and Mr. Wesley, they would then be held accountable and would provide such simple structures as were needed to undergird the covenant.

During the conference, methods of teaching and preaching were also discussed. How could they share the gospel in their specific context? What was essential and what would work? What methods would be faithful to the nature of the church and still respond to their unique situation?

These spiritual ancestors were exploring new methods. Experimentation within a valued heritage became their mode. Thus was the beginning of the evolving United Methodist annual conference.

There is a major difference between "conferencing" and "legislating." Conferencing as a style implies open and respectful sharing of ideas and experience as we seek for the better wisdom. As our church has grown larger and more complex, it was thought that our conferences needed a legislative style. The new style requires parliamentary procedure, motions and amendments, debate and political coalitions. However, we are still at our best when we follow the spirit of "conferencing."

Hidden in every conference discussion is the question: "What to teach?" Every recommendation, each proposal, all motions and speeches are built on some assumption about the nature of the Christian faith. These assumptions are worth listening for and identifying because the validity of what happens depends upon the assumptions. Our decisions are a part of our teaching, indeed, as is the debate itself. If one desires to understand the commitment and basic values of a gathering of persons, one has only to listen to the content and spirit of the debate.

Despite all the changes across the years, covenants still hold us together and define our life. These covenants are evident in the vows and commitments of membership, baptism, ordination, and consecration. However, the entire content of what we call *The Book of Discipline* is covenantal, covenants decided upon by our representatives at General Conference. Our tendency to view this book as a collection of legislation and to put it together by legislative means is gradually weakening the power and significance of the content. By their nature, covenants are more binding than laws for they grow out of the essence of Christian community.

A similar weakening is evident in many annual conferences. We have convinced ourselves that we can do whatever we vote on. In the absence of compelling purpose and agreed upon focus, annual conferences have proliferated organizational structures and multiple projects. Any compelling speech on the floor of annual conference can easily result in another such project. As a consequence, many good things have been tried and accomplished. The resources of our congregations are more and more dissipated. This habit of life increasingly denies us the power of focused effort and concentrated deployment of resources.

The United Methodist Church seems to reflect whatever attitudes or values exist in the surrounding culture. Thus, rampant individualism decays our covenantal relationship as pastors and laity insist on personal advantage and minimal accountability. Growing cynicism about the trustworthiness of political and business leadership immediately attaches itself to any strong church leader. Localism and self-interest create resistance for any effort that does not produce an identifiable profit for the individual contributor or "my congregation."

How may an annual conference radiate vision, purpose, and vital faith? In what way may an annual conference be formed so that the entire church will respond to the fire of God's passionate mission?

Fire of God's Passionate Mission

The nature of the question conditions the quality of the answer. The church is the Body of Jesus Christ. To frame this question adequately, one must humbly sit in the presence of the annual conference and ponder: "These annual conferences are a part of the Body of Christ. The spirit of Christ is in this body. This alone requires that we focus our contemplation, listening for the Creator groaning as something new seeks to be born. What is it that the Christ desires from these annual conferences? How should they be formed and shaped to be more adequate vessels?"

I learned this imagery from a Benedictine monk who was trying to teach me the skills of pottery. I had gone to him because I desired to make a chalice. As my instruction progressed, I found myself one day sitting at a potter's wheel. On it was unshaped clay. I had been taught to wet my hands and gradually draw out of the clay the shape of a chalice as the wheel slowly turned. Sensitive fingers were guided by the vision of a chalice, feeling the imperfections of the clay and using them so that they added to the chalice and did not create weakness. This was a very frustrating experience. I repeatedly failed.

At one point, this gentle friend said to me, "David, watch your hands and tell me what you are learning about God." I was frustrated at my inability and increasingly irritated. The last thing I wanted to hear was his comment. Then came the gift of insight.

The wet hands of God gently and skillfully work with the clay of my life seeking to draw out of me a useful vessel. God senses my imperfections and weaknesses and utilizes them so that they add strength and I, the clay,

yielding, participating, even anticipating the vessel God would have me be.

In that spirit we ponder the future of our annual conferences. How is God seeking to form and shape us? What sort of vessel are we to be? For what purpose are we being formed?

Because this bishop believes that annual conferences have a critical role to play in the creation of missionary congregations with missionary leaders, I offer these beginning thoughts:

1. Centers of celebration: Whether in large annual conference gatherings or district rallies, celebration, worship, and inspiration are agenda of the highest order. We celebrate our identity: we are the Body of Christ! We sing, we experience Bible study together, the Word is preached, the Sacraments are present, and we acknowledge God's presence. Many of our people worship in congregations numbering seventy-five or less. Seldom do they experience the power of a large gathering of Christian people celebrating the faith. On these occasions, we all are freshly claimed by Jesus Christ and the larger company of God's people.

2. A network of connections (signs of God's wet hands at work): Connection and mutual resourcing are gifts of the annual conference.

(A) Clusters of congregations are being formed at an amazing rate. Still maintaining their individual identity, congregations are discovering that they can resource one another. Each congregation has persons of skill or ability who can be shared with others. There are cooperative ministries that many congregations could never do alone. Some clusters combine their financial resources to make possible the kind of productive staffing found so helpful in larger congregations.

(B) Connections of clergy such as cluster groups, Bible study groups, Covenant Discipleship groups, fellowship and recreation provide strength and encouragement to the frequently isolated and stressed clergy.

(C) The annual conference provides connection for the congregations with global needs, helping our people focus their compassion and learn from Christian colleagues.

3. Centers of leadership development, deployment, and accountability: In the early days of our church, in bishops and presiding elders, there clustered powerful forces that were the fire of our movement. These early leaders provided oversight, the earliest forms of continuing pastoral education, modeling, constant communication of vision, the planting of congregations, accountability, and evangelical energy that created a contagious imperative. They recruited, trained, and deployed congregational leadership in order that the movement would continue to grow and persons would continue to be drawn into relationship with Jesus Christ. We still have an urgent need for this dynamic. If we are to be a church ready for its future, our annual conferences will once again take up this imperative as a matter of first priority.

Cabinets Sharpen Their Focus

The quality and focus of an annual conference cabinet are important to the question of this chapter. I reflect on this fact from the perspective of three much appreciated annual conferences and their cabinets. At the meeting of one of those cabinets, I looked down the table and was sobered by what I saw. The cabinet was busy at its task. Conversation was intense, at times punctuated by moments of laughter, and filled with words about mission. The agenda included worship, sharing of joys and concerns of parsonage families and others, appointments, apportionments, programs needing support, personnel problems, and leadership development.

I observed something else: weary eyes and long sighs. I knew that cabinet members had attended too many meetings, absorbed too much criticism, and worked too many days without time off. I knew the symptoms. I became a district superintendent in 1972. Since that time, despite several intervening years as pastor of a local church, I have worked with eighty-one different cabinet members. The fatigue lines observed on this particular day were on all eighty-one of those faces. All United Methodist members have their own list of what cabinet members must do, and each of those lists is a little different. It is easy to be overwhelmed by the expectations, pressured into trying to do everything.

It is time for cabinets to narrow their focus. I am convinced that cabinet members have six primary responsibilities. Other things need to be done and will be done. These purposes are fundamental.

1. Spiritual guides and teachers. Each cabinet member is a Christian person, growing in faith, and ready to encourage others in faith formation. They will help congregations identify themselves as centers of faith development. They will be "companions of the way" with pastors.

2. Pastoral oversight of both congregations and pastors. Cabinet members are to be persons who lift high the vision of a church in mission and assist congregations in fulfilling that mission. They will be encouragers, hope-carriers, guides, and representatives of accountability. Their major focus is on strengthening congregations and congregational leaders. Time spent with congregations will be their best time.

3. Resource persons, consultants, information carriers. All cabinet members will have gifts unique to themselves. Where their insight or knowledge is helpful, they will share it. When they are not prepared to assist directly, they will seek to identify persons or resource material that will address the need. Like their early predecessors, they will seek to be walking libraries of needed information.

4. Embodiment of the Connection. Through their own faith commitment, knowledge of The United Methodist Church, and presence among the people, cabinet members are interpreters and tellers of the story. In the long history of this unique office, these persons have always been a part of the glue that has held the Connection together.

5. The global Connection. Cabinet members help link each congregation with the global mission of our church.

6. As a total cabinet, they share with the bishop in the temporal and spiritual oversight of the annual conference. This leadership responsibility requires that they articulate a clear vision of our mission and be comprehensively informed about the goals and activity of the annual conference and its districts. They will assist in the placement of pastors using missional criteria for the making of appointments.

It should be noted that cabinets now include district superintendents, Council on Ministries director, and the conference administrator/treasurer. This expansion of cabinet membership has greatly enriched the potential for creative leadership and oversight. These persons must lead the way as our church is formed by God for its future mission responsibility.

We Are in the Congregation Business

When one examines annual conferences and cabinets, there is an additional issue too compelling to ignore. It can be illustrated with this conversation:

"Do you have a minute to visit? I would like to ask you something. What do you mean when you say that evangelism involves starting new churches?" This question was asked at the conclusion of a district rally. I responded by saying, "A principle method of evangelism in Christianity has been the starting of new congregations. That has been the basis of the rapid expansion of our faith around the world. New Christians were immediately connected with a congregation. Christians who moved to a new place sought out a congregation. If no parish was available, one was started without delay."

The tone of the person's response was surprise and concern. "I thought you would say that evangelism is one Christian sharing his or her faith with another. What about personal evangelism?" A worthy question! So I continued: "Personal evangelism, always present, was a means of extending the invitation to follow Christ and connect with Christ's church. Preaching also was very significant as was the quality of life of the Christian people. People were drawn to congregations because of the courage and love of the members." You may have heard the quote: "My, how these Christians love one another."

My persistent friend continued: "If the starting of new congregations is so important, why have I not heard more about it?" This was an exciting exchange. I said: "Please read the book of Acts. The disciples traveled to new communities, preached the gospel, and immediately started a congregation. Leaders were chosen, instructed, and left in charge of further spiritual and numerical growth. Congregation by congregation, Christianity spread south into Africa, east into Asia, and north into Europe. Christians have always been people of the congregations."

"Has this kind of evangelism been true of our United Methodist history?" I was asked. "Yes. One of the primary responsibilities of the early district superintendents (presiding elders) was the starting of churches. It was said that no sooner had a pioneer family begun to clear land for a cabin and farm than a circuit rider would appear. The question was always the same: 'Would you be willing to invite the neighbors to a preaching service in your cabin?' Our church spread across the North American continent congregation by congregation. That's how The United Methodist Church in your town got there."

This conversation was not over. "In modern times, haven't our methods of evangelism changed? Personal evangelism and church growth techniques seem to be dominant in our literature and church programs." My questioner was a reliable observer. The individualism of North American culture has dominated our perception of evangelism. The culture of consumerism has informed some of the church growth material. Despite these influences, both one-to-one evangelism and the church growth movement have been very helpful. However, most of our people have missed one critical fact. Protestant denominations that have concentrated on new church starts have grown. The United Methodist failure at this point is one of the reasons we have not been growing in recent times in the United States.

Now the telling point. "But we have so many churches now. Don't we have enough? Our buildings have plenty of room, and we have good programs."

I hope my questioner caught the sense of urgency in my reply: "Every United Methodist congregation is in mission. Outreach and meeting the needs of persons must be central to our life. In addition, wherever there is a new concentration of people, a new church is needed. People who have not been part of the Christian faith find new congregations attractive. You will want to know that starting a new congregation seldom detracts from the ministry of churches already there. The new congregation simply results in an increased number of persons being reached for Jesus Christ."

In keeping with our history, responsibility for starting new congregations resides with our district superintendents. They work in cooperation with the research and funding agencies of the annual conference. We all confess the scarcity of funding for new church starts. However, the gospel imperative will not release us. We have a great need for creative ideas about how congregations can be planted in ever increasing numbers. We must not be distracted from this responsibility. The need is compelling.

CHAPTER SEVEN

A Global Church: Compassion, Peacemaking, and Healing

A clue to understanding the nature of The United Methodist Church is found in *The Book of Discipline* (pars. 208-214). We are an inclusive fellowship of believers who profess our faith in God, in Jesus Christ, and in the Holy Spirit. In the vows of membership we make this affirmation and declare our desire to live our daily lives as disciples of Jesus Christ. We covenant together with God and other church members to keep these vows and to be loyal to The United Methodist Church, upholding it by our prayers, presence, gifts, and service. These are paragraphs worthy of study and discussion in each congregation.

One of these defining statements is paragraph 210: "A member of any local United Methodist Church is a member of the total United Methodist connection." One of the gifts we give our members is "global citizenship." There are annual conferences and congregations around the whole earth. In each place the culture is distinct and the language different. Each of these annual conferences and congregations has equal standing in the denomination. When persons unite with a United Methodist congregation any place in the world, we help them understand that they are in that instant a full member in covenant relationship wherever United Methodists are found.

Africa, for Example

The Council of Bishops is a faithful expression of our global nature. When it meets, bishops attend from around the planet. Just as clergy hold their church membership in the annual conference, the church membership of bishops is in this council. Regardless of their place of service, bishops are in a covenantal, congregational relationship with one another. Working together in the council, bishops fulfill their oversight responsibility for The United Methodist Church. They also provide mutual support and encouragement through worship, covenant groups, occasional training events, and friendship. Occasionally, the council also gives assignments to its members beyond the residential/presidential assignments given by jurisdictional and central conferences.

The following vignettes of global United Methodism come from the life of our bishops and from the context of these council assignments. I have chosen these as illustrations for they are ones in which I have directly participated. Any one of our bishops could provide a similar set of observations.

1. Bishop Alfred Ndoricimpa is a courageous and deeply committed Christian who led his church in Burundi to join The United Methodist Church in 1984. Bishop Emilio de Carvalho of our church in Angola helped guide this process and served as advisor to Bishop Ndoricimpa. The next year I was sent to Burundi on the first episcopal visit from the Council of Bishops. As always, the purpose of the visit was to support Bishop Ndoricimpa, to learn of the ministry of the church in Burundi, and to respond to requests for assistance. This was the beginning of a good friendship.

The Burundi Annual Conference and Bishop Ndoricimpa had an extensive and growing ministry. Church member-

ship was growing. There was major emphasis on health
care and education, especially the education of pastors.
The church was also a major supporter of the democracy
movement in this troubled land. This last fact was a source
of difficulty and constant threat. Finally, in 1994, antidemo-
cratic forces so threatened the life of our bishop that the
council sent two of us on an accompaniment mission.
Bishop Walter Klaiber of Germany and I spent time visiting
our bishop to signal that he was an international figure and
should not be harmed.

Like many African church leaders, Bishop Ndoricimpa
moved with remarkable indifference to his own well-being
by continually visiting the church across Burundi. It was
not unusual for people, who were in exile across nearby
borders, to risk reentry into Burundi just to see the bishop.
One of the district superintendents said: "Our people feel
safe when our bishop comes." I suggested that the bishop
could not prevent a hostile army from harming them. The
superintendent replied: "You do not understand. I speak of
spiritual safety. That is what is important."

Was the threat real? On the evening before our depar-
ture, we enjoyed an evening meal with Bishop Ndoricimpa
and several leaders of the annual conference. We spoke of
the future, of the mission of the church in Burundi, and
security issues for the bishop. After we left the restaurant,
military personnel, who had obviously been watching,
came to the restaurant and killed all the waiters who had
provided our meal. Just a warning, it was said.

2. A leading United Methodist bishop in Africa is Bishop
Emilio de Carvalho of Angola. Again, our church was a
leading advocate of liberation from colonial oppression in
Angola, and Bishop de Carvalho, then a young pastor, paid
a great price for his leadership. He finally escaped prison
with its abuse and torture and eventually arrived in the
United States. Our friendship began when Emilio became

my roommate at Garrett Biblical Institute (now Garrett-Evangelical Theological Seminary) in the 1950s.

The devastating civil war in Angola became far more difficult when the results of democratic elections were violated by the losing side and military conflict restarted. Whole villages fled from the fighting zone. Thousands of misplaced or orphaned children appeared in the capital city of Luanda. Bishop de Carvalho had led The United Methodist Church in Angola to a position of strength and strong leadership development. Now that annual conference faced a demanding situation. With little outside help, the church established missions in refugee camps, reorganized the congregations among the villagers who had fled to new locations, and began the process of health care and education for thousands of homeless children in Luanda.

Mrs. de Carvalho challenged the United Methodist Women in each congregation to start a childcare center. At the end of a Sunday worship service, I saw members immediately move furniture and equipment so they could again feed and teach the street children. Families whom the civil war and runaway inflation had left with little resources sacrificed to make this ministry possible. And still, the number of homeless children grew. In the evenings, I would walk the streets of Luanda to see children, with no source of food, sleeping in churchyards and beside city buildings. Preteen girls sought to survive through prostitution. The conference lay leader is a nurse. She helped some of the younger girls deal with venereal disease and find better solutions for their survival.

3. Liberia has been torn apart by conflicting factions seeking control. Monrovia is a bombed out city. United Methodist schools and hospitals have been destroyed in several locations. Liberians have fled to neighboring countries. Several annual conferences in the United States have been blessed by the strong ministry of Liberian pastors who were forced to flee for their lives. Yet, again and again,

our church in Liberia has marshaled its strength and reestablished its ministry to the people. Bishop Arthur Kulah has continued to risk himself on behalf of the mission. Several years ago, he spoke on national radio condemning the oppression of the government of Samuel Doe. Bishop Kulah continues to work for the establishment of free elections and a government chosen by the people. I have been with him when he has calmly faced a government official who was threatening him with immediate harm. Like other African bishops and church leaders, he remains faithful to the mission of the church in complex and demanding times.

Every United Methodist who reads these pages is a member of each congregation in these African nations and all other United Methodist congregations wherever they are found. Global membership is not just an interesting theory. Our members are cheated when they are not told about the special nature of their church membership. Effective servant leaders in congregations make a list of all the nations where our people are found in order to help their own members visualize the full scope of their membership.

Economics Leads the Way

Despite the frequent pull of nationalism, global economic forces are less and less concerned about national boundaries. A few years ago we were getting used to the term "multinational corporations." The phenomenon was new and many books were written about the positive and negative effects of these corporations. Now, the presence of global business organizations seems so normal when one hears that phrase. Business headquarters are located at sites of convenience. Political factors and national boundaries are concerned only to ensure reasonable safe stability. It is almost meaningless to refer to the national origin of a product. For instance, parts for so-called American automobiles are manufactured all over the world and shipped to the point of assembly. That point of assembly could easily be Canada or Mexico. The finished product is shipped into the national boundaries of the United States and sold as an American automobile. Automobiles with Japanese sounding names are built with similar parts around the world and assembled in the United States by American laborers. Still, we refer to these as Japanese. There are few products that escape this global flavor.

Expansion of economic coalitions and common markets is another example of the weakening of national boundaries. The development of the European Common Market struggles toward its fulfillment. While maintaining national identity, there is simultaneous promise of common passports, open borders, free trade agreements, coordinated economic policy, and the possibility of a common currency. The Pacific Rim Nations are rapidly evolving similar economic coalitions. Taiwan and South Korea are beginning to parallel the economic power of Japan as the financial centers of Hong Kong, under the influence of the 1997 return to China, begin to diminish. The North American Free Trade Agreement involving Mexico, Canada, and the United States has made its faltering start.

On the surface, continual splintering and reshaping of national boundaries, especially in Eastern Europe, might suggest a turn from this global direction. However, when one's attention shifts from newspaper headlines to the economic pages, one discovers that the trend continues in force. Despite the unpopularity of the United States in many parts of the world, the participation of our economic and business leaders in this global trend is vigorous and welcomed.

Communications Creates the Climate

With the exception of different electrical voltage and the occasional need to step up into the bathroom or bathtub, hotel rooms around the world look much alike. When you wake up in the morning, it's difficult to tell where you are. Walk across the room and turn on the television and you find a familiar logo. The CNN reporter and photographer are there to greet you. As satellite reception of television and radio signals continues to expand, one can find battery-operated televisions in remarkable places viewing the same CNN programs. Instead of waiting for airmail or letters carried by ships, the world population now experiences immediate involvement in world affairs. The television camera gives you real time exposure to military action in the Middle East, Eastern Europe, and Africa. Speeches by world leaders and dramatic shifts in world politics have a world audience. Powerful shortwave radio signals make available BBC's reliable news coverage and on-site radio interviews. Even a person as unsophisticated in computers as this writer has free and regular Internet communication with persons around the world.

We are raising our children in a communication environment radically different from that most of us experienced. They have reason to assume that the world is at their fingertips. They are subject to the pain and joys of global citizenship. For them, national boundaries are not high walls over which one cannot see and which one regularly mounts to fight off some enemy. Rather, these boundaries have a filmlike character through which one can easily see and pass. A church and an educational system that do not prepare them to live in this larger world, to speak its languages, to understand and appreciate its cultures, and to think critically about what they see and hear fail these young people in their preparation for their new and different citizenship.

Learning from Contextualized Theology

The theological orientation of the Western world has been dominant for a long time. Parts of the world colonized by Western thinking and teaching look upon this faith perspective as normative. We conclude that it is not only valid for us but also valid for all people everywhere. We acknowledge with difficulty that these Western theological assumptions represent a contextualized Christianity. After all, this is our normal culture, our worldview. Why would not everyone understand Christianity this way? The great missionary effort of the past and present is conditioned by Christianity contextualized in the Western world. For that reason, the faith we shared was Western Christianity. It was genuine gospel. Lives were transformed because of it. Its teachings about the dignity and worth of individuals helped fuel liberation movements. At the end of the day, mature Christians around the world began to realize that they now needed to allow the Christian faith to interact with their own cultural and religious context.

Liberation theology of Latin America was one such struggle. Christians read the Scripture and contemplated the basic wisdom of the Christian movement from the context of their real-life situations. The result was powerful. Asian Christians have entered a similar yet different theological adventure. Some of the world's most ancient religions are found there. What is the result when biblical Christianity dialogues with the wisdom of these other religions? How does the faith best express itself in that dialogue? The determination to contextualize Christianity in the Chinese experience, thereby breaking the control of Western Christianity, is one example. Again, a similar but different theological adventure is found in Africa. Unique cultures and a variety of religious expressions were devaluated in the great missionary expansion. Now African theologians are exploring Christian theology from the perspective of their own context.

In all these regions of the world, Christianity in its variety of settings now encounters a new missionary phase in Islam. Africa, Europe, and the United States are seeing an expansion of Islam unmatched in modern history. It is generally agreed that Islam is the fastest growing religion in the United States. The Muslim faith is a spiritual cousin of Christianity and Judaism. Outside the spotlight of angry international politics, a thoughtful conversation is taking place about the meaningful points of intersection between these three religions of Abraham. This conversation and all the others have little to do with national boundaries. From ancient times we have known that nations come and go but the people of God live on.

Active Recognition of Our Global Nature

The global definition of our United Methodist membership is a great gift. Our people have a faith relationship with persons on every part of this planet. When we watch television or read newspapers and magazines, we understand that there is no place so distant from us, no people so different from us, no problems so remote to our life experience or interests but what our active Christian compassion can immediately respond. Those are our people. The circumstances they face are of concern to us. What they are learning about faithful discipleship we need to know. We want to share any gift God has given us that might prove helpful to them. Is this a United States voice speaking? Yes, but more! These are now and will increasingly be the voices of United Methodist people worldwide. We all have gifts to share with the entire family.

A second active response to our global nature will prove more difficult. As a function of numerical strength and a lingering colonial attitude, The United Methodist Church has been dominated by the annual conferences in the United States. No greater evidence can be seen of this than the General Conference held quadrennially. The struggle is constant to keep that global gathering global in its orientation. Legislative proposals and social concerns resolutions usually speak to conditions and needs in the United States. Given what has been said above, it is legitimate to say that United Methodists from other parts of the world can appropriately participate in making these decisions out of their concern for the well-being of their brothers and sisters in the United States. However, the domination in both numbers and Western Christian orientation is not defensible. What we search for is a way of maintaining the integrity of our global connection at the same time that we celebrate and enable the regionalization of our church.

Every region of the world has its unique characteristics and needs. We have already pointed to the contextualization of Christian theology as fertile ground from which we all can learn. Regional gatherings of United Methodist people have the rightful responsibility to make decisions pertaining to their part of the world, shaping mission in ways their life experience deems wise. The General Conference, by logical extension, can be formed in new ways. With equal representation from all parts of the world, United Methodist people come together to maintain the Connection, to make strategic decisions about mutual ministry and mission, and to focus our global resources on issues and needs we may all address in concert. The specifics of this new United Methodist Church are yet to be discovered. The discovery is urgent.

The Global Call for a Passionate People

What is now cannot be the future! We must search for companions, persons of passionate spirit and wisdom, who will share our hunger for a different world.

1. Persons of passionate spirit and wisdom are those who love God with their minds. In cultures absorbed with self and becoming increasingly parochial, there is a great need for persons of insatiable curiosity, persons who are hungry to understand. All life is interconnected. We are increasingly global citizens. This passionate person will read and learn from diverse resources so as not to be captured by editorial positions or convenient political bias. We are being called to stop being tourists and become participant observers in life. Heart and mind join forces as

we seek to remain engaged with the human condition in all parts of the world.

2. I am convinced that our intellectual curiosity will make historians of us. In a recent flight at 35,000 feet, I discovered you could see the patterns of former river beds, the locations of now abandoned roads and trails, the flow patterns of the most recent floods. Imprinted on the earth was its ancient and modern history. A similar imprinting is recorded in our history, our stories: the wisdom of the ancient ones, the decisions and actions that conditioned events, the climate and social customs of all our people that have helped to shape the current change. Persons of passionate spirit and wisdom read the signs and better discern the nature of life now surrounding us.

3. One recalls T. S. Eliot's question: "Where is the wisdom we have lost in knowledge, where is the knowledge we have lost in information?" It is said that this is the information age. Yet the least informed person intuitively knows that information is not enough. A major problem in higher education is that we have inherited the tradition of learning only as utilitarian but have lost the tradition of learning as the seedbed of wisdom. In order to move into our missionary future we will need to prepare leaders who understand that every significant question involves values, a sensitivity to the mystery of life, and a passionate concern for the human condition. Persons of passionate spirit and wisdom will seek freedom from ignorance and prejudice, will sense the continuities and interconnectedness in life. Such persons face life's ambiguity and understand the persistent presence of evil as a part of the human dilemma. There is in the Christian faith an untempered awareness that life is not always kind. Sometimes the struggles seem impossible, and the efforts to be loving and healing can lead to a cross. Many of our United Methodist colleagues have seen evil close up.

The person of passionate spirit and wisdom is a carrier of values, one who will continue to offer gifts of liberation and encouragement, even when all about them is difficult. In this violent, competitive, and macho world there is a scarcity of gentle people, the compassionate ones, the peacemakers. Institutions and organizations do not contain their own values. Values are always carried in from the outside. Every corporation, every local business, every organization is an arena of value conflict. Life has a right to expect of us that we shall soon gain clarity about the primary values and faithfully carry them into the human enterprise.

4. Now we must address the most difficult passion of all. It has taken many of us years of struggle with the Christian faith finally to understand. The person of passionate spirit and wisdom is one who shares God's love affair with the poor. This is a constant theme in the whole of the Scripture. When we stare into life's face, staring back at us are masses of persons living along the edge, surrounded by forces outside their control, condemned by culture, family heritage, limited education, and misuse of life. Those who have no voice need us to be their voice. A culture that values things and uses people needs to be challenged by those of us who have compassionate impatience, who will ask why these conditions must exist, and what beginnings can be made to open doors to the future.

The person of compassionate spirit and wisdom is clear that graft and corruption, undisciplined profit seeking, and indifference are the jailers of far too many of us. We global United Methodists with a whole world in our hearts have questions to ask and answer: Who among us will seek to break the cycle of poverty? Who will lay aside false assumptions and engage in direct relationships that will bring understanding? Who will use their talent and influence to bring new hope to the children of the poor? Who will seek to influence international political and economic structures so that all may discover and enjoy the blessings of God? Who will carry this fire in their hearts?

CHAPTER EIGHT

Coming City of God's Shalom: Whispers of Hope

We end where we began. The church is compelled to respond to a change afoot. We travel through unfamiliar territory. Everything about us has the character of mission opportunity. We are to be missionary congregations with missionary leaders. What does that mean? How will God form the church for the future? Some past experience will prove useful. The stable point is the unchanged power of the gospel. Like the circuit riders of old, we are traveling across new territory where there is an incomplete map and only traces of roads. While many persons are printing road maps, all of them are guesswork. Some of this guesswork is well informed by persons with dependable and creative imaginations. All of it must be viewed as suggestion with possibility.

Is there a compass that will keep us pointed in the right direction? We need a compelling image! To that need this final chapter will speak.

It might be said that a congregation has a thousand tasks and activities but little sense of destiny!

It might be said that many congregations aimlessly wander through the days without much sense of urgency or direction!

It must be said that "the church is of God and will prevail until the end of time."

It might be said that one of the reasons our churches are characterized by buildings busy with outside groups is that we lack a purpose of our own and must depend upon the mission and purpose of others to justify our existence!

It must be said that "where the people lack vision they will perish."

There is a significant learning for us when someone asks: "What is your church like?" The answer is self-revealing. We will probably mention location, size of building and membership, participation in worship, budget, the number of programs, the busyness of our building, whether or not we are gaining or losing members. Interesting, indeed perhaps helpful. But there is a haunting absence in this response.

Two basic questions deserve the attention of all persons. First, "Who are we?" Reflection on that question requires one to look into the past, to remember our baptism, to remember the story of our people, to remember the teachings of the Scripture. Our identity grows out of our roots. The second is, "Why are we here?" To reflect upon this question requires a look into the future. We must contemplate what is God's purpose for creation, for the human race, for the church? *I am one of God's people, a baptized person who carries within myself a relationship with God. I am influenced by the stories of our movement. I am here to share obediently in the fulfillment of the purposes God has for this creation.*

The gospel of Jesus Christ and the teachings of the New Testament announce a future with the power to shape the present. It is the "end" of history, its final goal that lends shape and purpose, gives meaning to present life. There is little meaning to the present without a vision, a compelling image, which at least hints at history's destiny.

Christianity liberates us from a depressing circular view of history, that fateful notion that history constantly repeats itself in a meaningless cycle of events from which there is no escape. Scripture teaches that history has a destiny, a direction and an end. We study both the history of the past and of the future. Some people suggest this means an end in chronological time. At least as significant, history has a purpose, an intention in the mind of God, which destiny all creation groans to achieve. Each generation is invited to fashion the present in harmony with God's intentions for life.

I am convinced that The United Methodist Church will never experience the vitality for which we yearn or create excitement among our people unless we hear this whisper of hope from the future, the promise of Jesus Christ to bring to fulfillment the reign of God's shalom. When all other analysis is completed, this issue will still need to be joined. There will not be a fire in the bones of the church until it has an intimation of why God has given it existence. Only then will preaching be a holy word/event. Only then will ministry take on vitality. Only then will worship, including the Sacraments, be a genuine food for life and not just an attempt to entertain the people.

The Coming City of God's Shalom:
A Compelling Image

A central biblical concept is sometimes called the kingdom of God, which is one of the dominant teachings in Jesus' ministry. One discovers Abraham, who set out to seek "the city . . . whose architect and builder is God" (Hebrews 11:10). Most compelling of all is the New Testament conclusion with a powerful revelation referring to "the holy city, the new Jerusalem, coming down out of heaven from God" (Revelation 21:2).

The city of God is offered as a sign of what God intends for the fulfillment of history. This compelling image offers a powerful way for congregations to understand themselves as they prepare for the future. It offers a source of hope that will protect us from the tendency to trivialize. The image can be a remarkable gift that will help us address the question of "why" we are here and "how" we are to be formed for our ministry.

The last two chapters of our Bible announce the coming new creation called the city of God.

> **Then I saw a new heaven and a new earth; for the first heaven and the first earth had passed away, and the sea was no more. And I saw the holy city, the new Jerusalem, coming down out of heaven from God, prepared as a bride adorned for her husband. And I heard a loud voice from the throne saying,**
> **"See, the home of God is among mortals.**
> **He will dwell with them as their God;**
> **they will be his peoples,**
> **and God himself will be with them;**
> **he will wipe every tear from their eyes.**
> **Death will be no more;**
> **mourning and crying and pain will be no more,**
> **for the first things have passed away."**
> **And the one who was seated on the throne said, "See, I am making all things new." He also said, "Write this, for these words are trustworthy and true." Then he said to me, "It is done! I am the Alpha and the Omega, the beginning and the end. To the thirsty I will give water as a gift from the spring of the water of life. Those who conquer will inherit these things, and I will be their God and they will be my children."**

I saw no temple in the city, for its temple is the Lord God the Almighty and the Lamb. And the city has no need of sun or moon to shine on it, for the glory of God is its light, and its lamp is the Lamb. The nations will walk by its light, and the kings of the earth will bring their glory into it. Its gates will never be shut by day—and there will be no night there. People will bring into it the glory and the honor of the nations. But nothing unclean will enter it. . . .

Then the angel showed me the river of the water of life, bright as crystal, flowing from the throne of God and of the Lamb through the middle of the street of the city.

(Revelation 21:1-7, 22-27; 22:1-2)

This apocalyptic imagery seeks to articulate the intention of God for all of creation. This is the direction of history's movement. The intention is not just for the church's fulfillment. The entire human family and all the orders of creation are not only "groaning" for the fulfillment of this image, but also are promised by the Creator that the battle has been won, that the powers of decay and destruction will be defeated, and that God's perfect rule of shalom can be expected. A new order is being established by God. A new order has come (Isaiah 43:19).

"I am about to do a new thing; now it springs forth, do you not perceive it?" The city of God is a power already released in history. Jesus as Messiah came to make actual all that God had promised. The city of God (kingdom of God) is already among us and it is still coming. Every present moment is alive with this city's actuality and promise. There is no naïveté here. Christian eschatological thought makes a place for discontinuity, fulfillment through negation (like resurrection through crucifixion).

There is no promise of a continuous upward slope. There is an "in spite of" character in the biblical faith—real defeat, real tragedy, and real negation of human hopes. And yet, "in spite of" present frustration and diminished prospects, the business of life is supported by the promise of God to bring about the consummation of history through Jesus Christ. There is mystery. The cross, the resurrection are involved. The "how" and "when" of the matter we do not know. How and when are not the ultimate questions. The ultimate questions are "who" and "why." Our confidence is in the faithfulness of God.

The Church as a Prefiguring of the Coming City of God

These previous paragraphs were a way of reminding us all of this compelling image. Now we must relate our congregations to it. Let the matter be plainly named. Our church is not the city of God. When the perfect fulfillment of that destiny is achieved through the intervention of God's Spirit, we note that it does not provide for a temple in the city. There will not be need for one. The purpose of the church will have been fulfilled.

Then what are we to say? The church is the city of God in provisional form. We experience no call for renewal or reestablishment of something out of the past. The church, all of our congregations, are to be a prefiguring of the shape of things to come. Here our congregations can find genuine power. Within our congregations one can expect to discover imperfect reflections of this future, commitments to live according to the new order, and a desire to keep the vision alive.

The church is weak by most standards. While we are called to obey the great commission of Jesus, the temporal power of Caesar regularly seems to defeat us. No single congregation, no annual conference full of congregations, no ecumenical arrangement can succeed in producing the city of God even for an instant. We confess that hell itself cannot prevail against the church of Christ (Matthew 16:18). We also admit that the church of this moment, every institutional form of the church, always lives in a sinful shortfall with a constant danger of becoming lukewarm to be spewed out of the mouth of God (Revelation 3:16).

Despite these limitations, the scriptural expectation is that the church in all of its forms and expressions will be a sign and promise of the assured coming of the perfect reign of God. This compelling image, the light of this expectation, invites our congregations to reexamine their life together. Pastors scrutinize preaching and worship services. Committees evaluate the appropriateness of activities. We wonder: Is our congregation motivated by a commitment to be a prefiguring of the coming city of God's shalom? Is it this vision that defines our sense of purpose? Is our life together in harmony with such vision? Do members of our congregation seek to help the whole human society move in that direction? The church is no ordinary human organization. We are a creation of God with a remarkable purpose. Our present moment is to be informed by this vision. We can reasonably expect to see signs of the eventual fulfillment in the ordinary life of our annual conferences and their congregations.

In the Meantime

What is invited now is imaginative contemplation. The missionary congregation can find its way by exploring the implications of this vision. We are introduced to the term *eschatopraxis*, that is, the doing of the future in the present. We seek our interim identity.

1. "The home of God is among mortals." Once a congregation gains some intimation of the presence of God's spirit, that congregation is forever thereafter compelled to examine its ministry with a sense of awe and wonder. The Incarnation reminds us that God again and again chooses to be among ordinary people. In the coming city of God's shalom, all ordinary people will be extraordinary because of God's grace. Today's congregation expresses this evaluation through a climate of mutual respect and an awareness that all persons are precious in God's sight. All the "isms" that divide us crash to their destruction against this rock. Clergy professionalism cannot survive in this climate. Every layperson discovers vocation and every pastor reclaims her or his ordination under the fresh awareness that the great and holy God has chosen to dwell among us.

In every moment of history there have been those who conclude that most persons were meant by nature to be slaves, the hewers of wood and the drawers of water. They existed simply to serve the needs of the more cultured classes. Such a notion of humankind is absolutely repugnant in our congregations. No "slaves" exist in the city of God. Every person is valued, held to be precious, and affirmed as filled with potential. A part of our modeling and prefiguring shows in the way we nourish and encourage one another to fulfill our Christian vocations.

2. "God will wipe away every tear from their eyes . . . . Mourning and crying and pain will be no more." A compassionate and caring spirit will be developed in every congregation that sees this vision of the city of God as a part of its own destiny. Compassion involves a sensitivity to tears, mourning, and pain. Compassion fashions a passionate and caring response out of great concern for the persons in congregation and community. Servant leaders in the congregation will continually search for ways to create a climate of mutual support and healing. Our congregations will grow in sensitivity to the suffering of the entire world. Through study, pastoral preaching, and mission trips, the congregation will develop the same love affair God has for the poor and the outcast.

It can be taken as a generous gift from God that we cannot feel simultaneously all the pain of creation as can God. We could not stand that. We would go mad. Rather, God has allowed us to experience just enough of that pain to sensitize our compassion. We sense the many kinds of death experienced by persons; we see the great cost of class and social divisions. We confess the human need to divide ourselves into valued or devalued groups in order that we can feel good about ourselves by feeling badly about others.

In our congregations we ponder these questions: Whose eyes will be Christ's eyes seeing with depth the need about us? Whose voice will be Christ's voice calling to the potential in each person, disclosing its presence and encouraging its practice? Whose gift of pastoral leadership will be Christ's pastoral concern creating a context in which persons can hear God calling their name? In the name of Christ, who will be the midwives among us to help persons give birth to their own futures? How will we open doors, affirm by awareness, provide study and learning experiences, and give permission and encouragement? How will we heal the congregation's tendency to mistreat, control or manipulate?

3. "To the thirsty I will give water as a gift from the spring of the water of life." Our missionary congregations are to be water carriers. We are surrounded by persons who have a great need for liberation from the things that bind and hurt. Persons need to forgive and be forgiven. The emptiness in life needs to be dealt with. The "water" we carry is a witness to God's grace, a pointing of people toward the fountain of God's "water of life."

4. "For he looked forward to the city that has foundations, whose architect and builder is God." If our congregations could be accused of any serious fault, it might be

the failure to share the Christian story with our own people. Like many of our institutions, our churches are drifting
toward the idolatry of the bottom line. We take our motives
and methods from the culture. It is well enough that the
number of participants does not fall and that people are
reasonably happy. Our prefiguring responsibility suggests
that persons participating in our congregations find themselves increasingly pointed toward "the architect and
builder" who is God.

5. A light to the nations—the healing of the nations.
This compelling image envisions assertive congregations
in a changing world. Our members know that their primary
citizenship is in God's city. These missionary congregations are called to be the conscience of the community.
Through prophetic efforts we seek to raise the moral and
ethical issues to new levels of awareness, to invite leaders
everywhere to be responsive to the needs of this world,
and to speak a good word on behalf of peace and healing.

CONCLUSION

Reflections in Bunhill Cemetery

Will anyone remember that we began this search for missionary congregations and missionary leaders? In prayer, we have started this journey trusting God and not knowing our exact destiny. Our vision has drawn us to both present service and continuing search. Ours is the forester's task. We will plant knowing that we will probably never see the result. Many of us will be retired long before God finally reveals the church's future form. Will anyone remember the vague hunger that motivated us?

A parallel consideration is: "What are the names of my great-great grandparents?" That may seem a strange question. It came to me as I was walking the pathways of Bunhill Cemetery in London. I was immersed at this center of the developing Methodist movement in England, with City Road Chapel, John Wesley's grave, and his three-story house, now a museum preserving his possessions across the street. Martha and I were living in a third-story apartment in Wesley's home. In England to give a series of lectures on the life and ministry of John Wesley to a group of traveling United Methodists, I had entered the Bunhill Cemetery at my first opportunity to search for two special graves.

An impressive monument marks the burial site of Sir Isaac Watts, author of many famous hymns. In contrast, a simple marker suggests the burial site of Susanna Wesley, John's mother. The cemetery sexton was a crusty character who gladly helped me find the graves. In subsequent days, he told stories about the politics of managing a famous cemetery and about the famous souls buried there. He also gave me permission to wander behind the gates into more remote sections.

At first these ancient headstones dating back 300 years fascinated me. I could hardly read the weathered lettering. Kneeling by the stone, I used my finger to trace letters. Who were these people? What could have been their story? The stones were frequently large. One could imagine mourners grieving during the rite of interment. They surely loved and respected the persons buried there. Now their identity was lost. The sexton had no record of their names. No family or friends came to remember. My fascination turned to sadness.

Then the question about my ancestors intruded into awareness. I didn't even know their names.

Leaning on a headstone, I heard a second humbling question: "Who will remember me one hundred years from now? Will anyone remember my story? What will remain of my life work?" I call the reflections of that day my Bunhill Insights.

Few persons, if any, will remember. That is a plain fact. All of us, great and small, will join that glorious category of "ancestors." Only three, sometimes four, generations can be present and remembered in any given moment.

God will know! God will remember! This is the only important answer. "Neither death nor life . . . can separate us from the love of God." God will love and appreciate us for all eternity.

This is the moment given by God. Our **now** is our missionary destiny, the arena for our contribution to the coming city of God's shalom. The Bunhill Insight frees us from concern for fleeting credit and short-lived reward. Our motive for service can be love of Christ with no strings attached. Our calling is to join with other Christians in seeking to form missionary congregations with missionary leaders.

The work of the faithful is never lost! Our service is remembered in its results. We build foundations on which others can stand. Our acts of mercy bear perpetual fruit. The knowledge we share influences life for multitudes. The witness Christ makes through us lives on for generations to come. The Bunhill Insight says that this is enough! Indeed, to serve well in the moment, giving more than we have ever given before, is to hear God's benediction: "Well done, good and faithful servant."